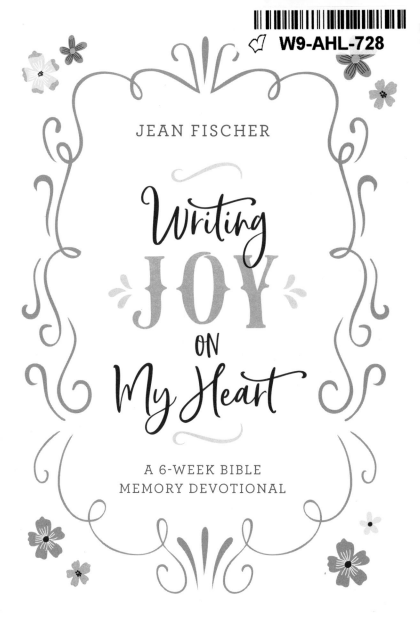

JEAN FISCHER

Writing JOY ON My Heart

A 6-WEEK BIBLE MEMORY DEVOTIONAL

BARBOUR BOOKS
An Imprint of Barbour Publishing, Inc.

W9-AHL-728

ISBN 978-1-64352-343-9

Published by Barbour Books, an imprint of Barbour Publishing, Inc., 1810 Barbour Drive, Uhrichsville, Ohio 44683, www.barbourbooks.com

Our mission is to inspire the world with the life-changing message of the Bible.

Member of the
Evangelical Christian
Publishers Association

Week 1
ON THE PATH TO JOY

Thou wilt shew me the path of life:
in thy presence is fulness of joy;
at thy right hand there are
pleasures for evermore.

PSALM 16:11

INEXPRESSIBLE AND GLORIOUS JOY!

Where are you on your path through life? Is there always joy in your heart? Dictionaries define *joy* as "a feeling of great pleasure and happiness." If you rely on that definition alone, you will discover that joy is fleeting. It is impossible to sustain that kind of joy 24-7.

Life's path, your journey from birth to death, is strewn with obstacles intended to steal your happiness. Satan will deliberately put roadblocks in your way. Jesus confirms this in John 10:10 (NKJV): "The thief does not come except to steal, and to kill, and to destroy." Satan's purpose is to steal joy—sustained feelings of great pleasure and gladness—and obliterate it.

Think of a time when the enemy stole your joy. Maybe it was through the death of a loved one, an illness, financial trouble, a job loss. . .he is always working to turn your happiness to despair. He loves when you give in to negative feelings, because in your weakness he gains strength.

What can you do to find sustainable joy? Follow Jesus! Allow Him to lead you, and you will have His kind of joy in your heart every day, every minute, of your life. Jesus says: "I have come that [you] may have life, and that [you] may have it more abundantly" (John 10:10 NKJV). When you welcome Him into your heart and trust Him to lead you, then you are on the path to true joy. As you read the Bible, soak up its words, and put them into action, you will see God's power working within you to overcome all obstacles in your way.

Do your best to be like Jesus. Read His words in the Bible. "These things," He says, "I have spoken to you, that My joy may remain in you, and that your joy may be full" (John 15:11 NKJV). His kind of joy is never ending.

Peter said this about Jesus: "Though you have not seen him, you love him; and even though you do not see him now, you believe in him and are filled with an inexpressible and glorious joy" (1 Peter 1:8 NIV). Jesus' presence in your heart is joy!

Writing Joy on My Heart is intended to lead you toward finding inexpressible and glorious joy every day, even on days when obstacles block your path.

Each week begins with a scripture memory verse. The tear-out index cards in the back of this book contain the verses to help you write each one on your heart. Daily devotionals explore the weekly verse in depth, illustrating how God's Word and its teaching affect your inner thoughts, salvation, eternity, relationships, and everyday life. Following each devotion is The Blank Page section where you will find ideas for applying what you've learned. And finally, The Last Word gives you even more to think about, digging deeper into words, ideas, scripture memorization, and more.

Let's see how you can apply today's devotion.

Thou wilt shew me the path of life: in thy presence is fulness of joy; at thy right hand there are pleasures for evermore.
PSALM 16:11

The Blank Page

To discover true joy, start small. Notice little things that make you smile. It might be a spontaneous hug from your son who thinks it isn't cool to hug his mom in public, or a kind act from a stranger, or the silly antics of a family pet. God works through others in small ways to help you see and appreciate the goodness around you. If you actively look for happiness in little things, you will begin to open your heart to never-ending joy.

You've heard it said, "Turn that frown upside down." How many times have you smiled today? On average, women smile sixty-two times a day (men only eight!). Getting into the habit of smiling can boost your mood. British researchers discovered that one smile stimulates the brain at the same level as two thousand chocolate bars! And smiles are contagious. Mother Teresa said, "Every time you smile at someone, it is an action of love, a gift to that person, a beautiful thing." Sharing your smile gives others a glimpse into your Jesus-filled heart. His presence within you shines outward through your smile. If you smile even when you're having a bad day, then you show others the Jesus kind of joy that breaks through whatever gets in your way.

Take time today to notice God's little blessings all around you—those things that make you smile. Then consciously and deliberately share your smiles with others. Share the inexpressible and glorious joy you've found knowing Jesus.

The Last Word

For some, memorizing scripture can be daunting. But it doesn't have to be. There are many different ways to commit a Bible verse to memory.

Repeating a verse is the key to writing it on your heart. Begin by using the Bible memory cards. Make each week's card an active part of your daily routine. Practice the verse in the morning while you put on makeup and do your hair. Take the card along to your workplace. Say the verse to yourself throughout the day, especially when negative feelings like frustration or boredom creep in. At bedtime, repeat the verse again. Allow it to run through your thoughts as you fall asleep.

Another technique is to analyze how the scripture applies to your life. Say the verse. Then meditate on what it means to you personally. Do this daily, thinking each day of a different way the verse affects you and where you are on your path.

If you enjoy art or crafts, create something using the daily verse. Or if music is your passion, turn the scripture into a song.

Pray the scripture. Recite it back to God. Ask Him to open your heart to the scripture's deeper meaning. Luke 24:45 says Jesus opened His disciples' minds to understand the scriptures. He will do that for you too!

Not everyone learns using the same method. Think about how you prefer to learn. Then list three ways that fit your own unique style.

Week 1: DAY TWO

THE LONG AND WINDING ROAD

The path through life is rarely smooth and straight. On your own path, you've likely encountered sharp turns, roundabouts, potholes, and detours. Did you face them joyfully? When getting from point A to B isn't easy, most people feel less than joyful. Some go on, moaning and complaining. Others come to a screeching halt or turn back. But a few praise God. They thank Him for their path even with its flaws. What reason do they have to be thankful? In a word: JESUS!

If you open your Bible and read Proverbs 3:5–6 (NKJV), you will discover how to find true joy wherever you are on life's path. It says, "Trust in the LORD with all your heart, and lean not on your own understanding; in all your ways acknowledge Him, and He shall direct your paths." In *all your ways* acknowledge Him! In other words, recognize Jesus' power and authority over *everything*, even the most mundane. Solomon wrote proverbs to offer instruction, wisdom, and understanding (see Proverbs 1:2). So think about his words in Proverbs 3:5–6. When the road is long and you feel tired, angry, frustrated, or defeated, ask Jesus to lead you. Allow Him to guide your path.

Trusting Jesus is the most important key to unlocking your heart so it can fill up with true, Jesus-inspired joy. When you

LOVE YOU

BEAUTIFUL

YOU ARE lovely

learn to trust in His unceasing presence in your life, you will experience comfort and reassurance knowing that everything is under control. He's got this! Your role is to permit Him to lead you and to have faith that He knows what He's doing. With Jesus in the driver's seat, you might still experience some quick turns and make several passes through the roundabout. But you can count on Jesus to get you safely onto a straight path and headed toward your destination—and that's reason enough to joyfully praise Him!

Some fitness centers have big street-side windows. When you drive by you can see people running on treadmills, watching the world pass by. Life can feel like that—you are marking time but going nowhere. Where's the joy in that? Real joy comes with remembering Jesus is present with you all the time. You don't have to figure out by yourself how to get back on the road and move toward your destination. Jesus is right there to help you. So get up and start walking.

Try to catch up to those further along on life's path. Ask their advice. God puts Christian friends on your path to help guide you to everyday joy that's rich and full. Traveling life alone isn't fun. When getting from point A to B becomes rough or tedious, remember Jesus is with you, and so are trusted friends who along the way will make you smile, laugh, and contribute to filling your heart with joy.

Thou wilt shew me the path of life: in thy presence is fulness of joy; at thy right hand there are pleasures for evermore.
PSALM 16:11

The Blank Page

Learning to trust Jesus means putting Him first.

Stop reading right now and make a list of the five most important things in your life. Rank them in order of importance. If you put Jesus/God at the top of your list, congratulations! He needs to be more important than your marriage, children, work, and yourself. Not putting Him first in everything allows the enemy to sneak in and seize your joy.

Incorporating spontaneous prayer into your everyday life is one way to gain trust in Jesus. Begin your day with a prayer. Then talk with Jesus throughout your day. Thank Him for little blessings you see. Ask Him to help you when negative feelings creep in. When you see someone who could use a little Jesus, ask Him to be with that person. If you do these things, you will learn that Jesus is there and trustworthy in all circumstances.

Another way to trust Jesus more is by journaling your faith. A faith journal is an ongoing love letter to the Lord. It's a place where you can pour out your frustrations, ask Him questions, reflect on your ever-growing faith, and keep a list of His blessings.

Immerse yourself in Jesus. Read the Bible, memorize scripture, read Christian books both fiction and nonfiction, look on the bright side of things, smile often, help others. . . these are all great ways to gain trust in Jesus and make Him most important in your life.

The Last Word

Pray the Twenty-Third Psalm paying close attention to the words in *italics*.

> The LORD is my shepherd; I shall not want. He maketh me to lie down in green pastures: *he leadeth me* beside the still waters. He restoreth my soul: *he leadeth me in the paths of righteousness* for his name's sake. *Yea, though I walk through the valley of the shadow of death, I will fear no evil: for thou art with me*; thy rod and thy staff they comfort me. Thou preparest a table before me in the presence of mine enemies: thou anointest my head with oil; my cup runneth over. Surely goodness and mercy shall follow me all the days of my life: and I will dwell in the house of the LORD for ever.

Now think about this week's memory verse, Psalm 16:11: "Thou wilt shew me the path of life: in thy presence is fulness of joy; at thy right hand there are pleasures for evermore." What does it have in common with the Twenty-Third Psalm? The theme of both is God's leadership and presence. Like the psalm says, He is our shepherd. With Him leading and caring for us, we can trust we have everything we need.

"O come, let us sing unto the LORD. . . . Let us come before his presence with thanksgiving. . . . For he is our God; and we are the people of his pasture, and the sheep of his hand" (Psalm 95:1–2, 7).

Week 1: DAY TWO

GOD CAN DO ANYTHING!

To trust God, you first need faith. Faith is believing God can do anything. Trust means willfully acting on your faith.

James wrote: "My friends, what good is it to say you have faith, when you don't do anything to show that you really do have faith? Can that kind of faith save you? . . . You surely believe there is only one God. That's fine. Even demons believe this, and it makes them shake with fear. . . . We please God by what we do and not only by what we believe" (James 2:14, 19, 24 CEV).

Acting on your faith can be as simple as asking for something in prayer and then trusting God's will for the answer.

Gladys Aylward served as a missionary in China during the first half of the twentieth century. During a tumultuous time of war between China and Japan, Gladys took in and cared for many orphaned children.

The fighting grew worse, and—having faith in God—Gladys went to her Bible searching for guidance. The book opened to Jeremiah 49. Her eyes rested on verse 30: "Flee, get you far off, dwell deep." She gathered the one hundred orphans in her charge, and with just a little grain for food, they began a long journey to safety in Siân.

The war left just one open route, a dangerous path over mountains and then across the Yellow River. When they arrived at the mile-wide river there were no boats. The Chinese soldiers had hidden them from the Japanese. Gladys didn't know what to do. But then, one of the children reminded her of God opening the Red Sea so Moses and the Israelites could cross. "God can do anything!" the little girl said. So Gladys and the children knelt and prayed, asking God for help. Before long a Chinese military officer arrived. When Gladys explained they were refugees fleeing the Japanese, the officer sent boats to carry them safely across the river.

Faith and trust are essential to finding true joy in the Lord. He is able to solve any seemingly insurmountable problem. Gladys, facing a grave situation, had slipped briefly into having faith without trust. It took a little child to remind her to reconnect the two and *do* something. There was nothing to do but pray. Still, that simple act brought results.

When you face obstacles on your path, have faith that God will help you. Sometimes all you can do is pray. Other times God will put it on your heart to trust Him and act in some specific way. But always, He will be there for you.

John H. Sammis, a Presbyterian minister and hymn writer, wrote this refrain in his well-known hymn "Trust and Obey":

> *"Trust and obey, for there's no other way to*
> *be happy in Jesus, but to trust and obey."*

Remember those words—and be happy in Jesus.

Thou wilt shew me the path of life: in thy presence is fulness of joy; at thy right hand there are pleasures for evermore.
PSALM 16:11

The Blank Page

When you ask God for help, He might send angels. Maybe they aren't angels in the true sense of the word, celestial beings appearing as human, but rather people God uses to work out His plan.

In Gladys Aylward's story, God sent a Chinese soldier to answer her prayer for help. Not just any soldier! God sent an officer who had authority to command that boats be brought so Gladys and one hundred children could cross to safety.

There are no coincidences.

Hebrews 13:2 says that some people encounter angels without even knowing. Have you been in a situation where someone showed up at the exact moment you needed something? Maybe you sat alone in a hospital room with a gravely ill loved one and a friend arrived to sit with and support you. Or maybe your car died on the freeway and a police cruiser just happened to be behind you.

When you read about Jesus you will discover He arrived at just the right time to fill a need. That is His promise to us. If we have faith, He will come—not as He did in His human Jesus body, but instead working through the hearts of people.

Today, notice Jesus in the actions of others: someone leaving a parking space just when you need one, or a store employee showing up with an item you were looking for. . . . Find joy in recognizing Jesus' faithful presence in your life.

The Last Word

Gladys Aylward was one of many missionaries around the world serving God, not only sharing the truth of Christ's salvation but also meeting the needs of others. Today there are nearly a half million Christian missionaries worldwide.

When you think of the word *missionary* you probably envision someone like Gladys, a person in a foreign country working to help its people while leading them to Christ. But a missionary doesn't have to travel to a faraway place to help others and share Jesus' love. There are missionaries in your own community, and you can be one of them!

Webster's defines *missionary* as "a person undertaking a mission." God gives each person different talents and skills he or she can use in service. If you ask God to reveal your mission or purpose, He will.

You can pray asking Him to lead you on a path to serve others. Listen to the ideas He puts in your heart. God may give you little missions where you serve for a day or a week volunteering at a food pantry, for example, or a fundraiser. Or He might give you a mission to bless others through words, art, or music. He might even set you on the path of a lifelong mission to serve Him in some big way.

Whenever you use your God-given talents and skills to serve others, you will discover the good and joyful results it brings—and that will increase your faith!

You prayed and asked, believed and trusted. Still, when you expected Him to be there, it felt like Jesus wasn't.

In John 11, Jesus and His disciples were away from the village of Bethany when Jesus' good friend Lazarus became ill. Lazarus's condition deteriorated, and his desperate sisters, Mary and Martha, sent for Jesus. They expected He would hurry to Bethany and heal their brother. But Jesus didn't show up, and Lazarus died.

Why? his sisters wondered. *Why didn't our friend Jesus come and heal our brother?* You might imagine how they felt. Disappointed, surely. Angry, maybe. And certainly without joy.

Meanwhile, Jesus had received their message. He told His disciples, "His sickness won't end in death. It will bring glory to God and his Son" (v. 4 CEV). The disciples expected Jesus to return to Bethany and heal Lazarus, but instead Jesus waited two days until He knew Lazarus had died. "I am glad that I wasn't there," Jesus told them, "because now you will have a chance to put your faith in me. Let's go to him" (v. 15 CEV). The disciples worried about going with Jesus to Bethany because Lazarus had been a beloved member of the community. People there were angry with Jesus for not showing up to heal him. They might want to kill Jesus, and His disciples too! So His disciples went unwillingly.

Lazarus was dead four days when they arrived in Bethany. Martha hurried to meet Jesus. She said, "Lord, if you had been here, my brother would not have died. Yet even now I know that God will do anything you ask" (vv. 21–22 CEV).

Yet even now. Even in the middle of her sadness and disappointment, Martha still had faith.

Jesus had something bigger and better in mind when He waited to return to Bethany. He was operating on "Jesus Time" and not time as the world knows it. He went to Lazarus's tomb, with a crowd of Bethanians following Him, and He prayed. When Jesus had finished praying, He shouted, "Lazarus, come out!" And Lazarus came out of the tomb alive and well (vv. 41–44).

In every situation Jesus shows up, but in His own time. If He doesn't arrive when you expect Him, it is because He has a better time and a better plan. It might be the reward of heaven for a sick loved one, a career move leading to something wonderful, a positive relationship change, or just to build up your faith. . . .

Is there joy when you need Jesus and He doesn't show up? Remember—joy is a feeling. Like all feelings it comes and goes. There is joy in knowing that Jesus *isn't* a feeling. *He* is your joy. True joy is believing Jesus has the best answer to your prayers. He is always with you, working on your behalf, and in the worst of circumstances helping to make you strong.

Thou wilt shew me the path of life: in thy presence is fulness of joy; at thy right hand there are pleasures for evermore.
PSALM 16:11

The Blank Page

James wrote, "Consider it pure joy, my brothers and sisters, whenever you face trials of many kinds, because you know that the testing of your faith produces perseverance. Let perseverance finish its work so that you may be mature and complete, not lacking anything" (James 1:2–4 NIV).

The apostle Paul put those words into action. His life path was strewn with trouble, illnesses, shipwrecks, riots, beatings, imprisonments. . .but he persevered, and that strengthened his faith. He wrote, "I have learned to be content whatever the circumstances. I know what it is to be in need, and I know what it is to have plenty. I have learned the secret of being content in any and every situation, whether well fed or hungry, whether living in plenty or in want. I can do all this through him who gives me strength" (Philippians 4:11–13 NIV). Paul shared his secret to contentment in 1 Thessalonians 5:18 (NIV): "Give thanks in all circumstances; for this is God's will for you in Christ Jesus."

Paul felt safe in the love of Jesus and sure of His continual presence. Even in the worst times, he had joy knowing he wasn't alone. You can have that kind of joy too! Start today thanking God in all circumstances. Trust in His perfect timing and His good plans for you. If you persevere, praising Him for His faithfulness, then your faith will grow, and you'll find contentment in all situations.

The Last Word

A helpful way to memorize scripture is to connect it with a story, image, or quotation.

As you think about the stories in this week's devotionals, make an effort to connect them with your memory verse, Psalm 16:11: "Thou wilt shew me the path of life: in thy presence is fulness of joy; at thy right hand there are pleasures for evermore."

Maybe a title created a picture in your head ("The Long and Winding Road," for example). Try connecting the words of Psalm 16:11 to that image.

You might remember a quote from one of the devotional readings. The orphaned child in Gladys Aylward's story saying, "God can do anything!" or James's words, "Consider it pure joy, my brothers and sisters, whenever you face trials of many kinds." You can connect those to the memory verse by weaving them into short personal prayers:

Dear God, I know You can do anything! "Thou wilt shew me the path of life: in thy presence is fulness of joy; at thy right hand there are pleasures for evermore."

Dear Jesus, thank You for reminding me to "consider it pure joy whenever I face trials of many kinds," because I know "thou wilt shew me the path of life: in thy presence is fulness of joy; at thy right hand there are pleasures for evermore."

Try using these connecting tools when memorizing scripture. Allow the combination of scripture, stories, images, or quotations to help you write God's words on your heart.

THE THREE P'S

Think about how you travel life's path. Are you running with earbuds in, soaking up tips from a self-help podcast—oblivious to what's around you? Maybe you're more of a stop-and-smell-the-roses kind of gal; with each step something new catches your eye—and shuts out everything else.

There's nothing wrong with running or stopping to smell the roses, but traveling your path too fast or too slow isn't good because it will distract you from what God wants you to see. God and Satan have few things in common, but one of them is subtlety. The things they set along your path can be inconspicuous. You need to travel evenly and carefully with your eyes open, avoiding Satan's ploys and embracing God's blessings.

You are a wise traveler when you walk life's path practicing the Three P's: prayer, patience, and praise.

Prayer always comes first and is essential to the other two. Jesus said, "Ask and it will be given to you; seek and you will find; knock and the door will be opened to you. For everyone who asks receives; the one who seeks finds; and to the one who knocks, the door will be opened. Which of you, if your son asks for bread, will give him a stone? Or if he asks for a fish, will give him a snake? If you, then, though you are evil, know how to give good gifts to your children, how much more will your Father in heaven give good gifts to those who ask him!" (Matthew 7:7–11 NIV).

Notice the Lord's promises to those who pray. When you come to God in prayer, His door is open to you. He promises to answer your prayer. In whatever way He answers, you are assured that it is the best answer according to His will.

As you travel life's journey, you should pray all the time believing that God hears and will answer.

The second P, patience, follows prayer. Second Peter 3:8 (NIV) says: "But do not forget this one thing, dear friends: With the Lord a day is like a thousand years, and a thousand years are like a day." Accept that God exists in a time zone beyond your understanding. He will require patience from you, because learning patience helps build your faith and leads to a place of contentment.

The final P is praise. Praise the Lord joyfully for His answers to prayer. Praise Him for the ways He blesses you on your path through life. Praise Him for helping you notice and avoid Satan's traps. Praise is like a love song to your heavenly Father. It shows you appreciate His goodness, grace, and mercy. James wrote: "Is anyone happy? Let them sing songs of praise" (James 5:13 NIV). Praise is easy when you are happy. But if you learn to praise God even when your road gets rough, then you are well on the way to true joy.

Thou wilt shew me the path of life: in thy presence is fulness of joy; at thy right hand there are pleasures for evermore.
PSALM 16:11

The Blank Page

Technology has taken us to a place of speed and convenience. With the push of a button we can get almost anything we want. We shop online and our purchases show up at our doors. Programmable pressure cookers produce meals in minutes. Smart speakers function as virtual assistants, reminding us of scheduled tasks, turning lights on and off, even telling jokes when we need a little joy! As wonderful as these time-saving devices are, a surge in impatience comes with them. We want everything *right now*, and that's why patiently waiting for God is so hard.

Having patience with Him takes practice. It begins with you identifying your feelings of impatience. Next, stop whatever you are doing and spend time in prayer. Ask God to help you wait. Then let go of your expectations and get out of your time zone. While you wait, remember God has the situation under control. You can't rush headlong into the future because *you* don't own time, *God* does! Trust Him to take all the time He needs.

Patience is an act of will and practice. You build it one step at a time. Practice patience in common everyday situations, while standing in the checkout line, for example, or while stuck in traffic. Be aware when you become annoyed or fidgety. Bring God into the situation through silent prayer. When you learn to be patient with Him, you will also be more patient with yourself and others.

The Last Word

Praise involves us coming to the Lord. Psalm 100:4 invites us into His kingdom: "Enter into his gates with thanksgiving, and into his courts with praise."

The word *praise* is sometimes used interchangeably with the word *worship*. The two are closely related, but there is a difference. Praise is showing appreciation to God for what He has done. Worship is honoring God for who He is—the Great I Am, our heavenly Father, the One and only God. Worship is reserved for God alone. He is the only One worthy of worship. But while worship is only for Him, praise is not. He encourages us to praise each other for good works and accomplishments.

Did you know God praises us when we please Him? His praise comes in the form of blessings. However, John 12:43 holds a warning about praise. It reminds us not to love praise from people more than praise from God.

The joyful expression "Praise God!" conveys either happiness or relief. A new mother might say "Praise God" after her long and painful labor has ended. But when she sees her healthy newborn child, she might exclaim, *"Praise God!"* in recognition of His wonderful gift.

Along with words, there are other ways to praise Him. You can praise God together with Christian friends (see Hebrews 2:12), with music and dancing (see Psalm 149:3), or show your appreciation to Him by lifting your hands toward heaven (see Psalm 134:2).

IN THE WILDERNESS

There are endless reasons to find joy in knowing God: the gift of His Son, Jesus; salvation and the promise of heaven; safety; health and healing; His goodness and good works; His grace and mercy. . .the list goes on. Freedom is another reason for joy. And we find joy in God's leadership.

One of the best illustrations of His leadership is the book of Exodus. Thousands of Israelites celebrated when God rescued them from four hundred years of slavery in Egypt. God chose Moses to lead the way out and went ahead, guiding him on the safest path to the Red Sea. "The LORD showed them the way; during the day he went ahead of them in a pillar of cloud, and during the night he was in a pillar of fire to give them light. In this way they could travel during the day or night. The pillar of cloud was always with them during the day, and the pillar of fire was always with them at night" (Exodus 13:21–22 NCV). With God leading, the Israelites reached the Red Sea. The Egyptian soldiers were in pursuit, almost catching up. So God made a dry path through the sea so the Israelites could cross. Then He closed the path, causing the sea to swallow the Egyptians, chariots and all. Free at last! The Israelites sang a joyful song to the Lord and praised Him (see Exodus 15:1–21).

God promised the Israelites a new home, "a land flowing with milk and honey." He had cleared their path to freedom. But although He had faithfully led them, never left them, and kept them safe, the Israelites thought God abandoned them as they traveled and encountered obstacles. They lost faith in God. Their trust weakened. The Israelites trusted in themselves more than in God, and because of that they wandered around in the desert for forty years! Had they held tight to their trust in Him, they might have arrived sooner in the Promised Land.

It has been more than three thousand years since the Israelites' exodus from Egypt, and yet we humans still make the same mistake of losing trust in God's leadership when trouble gets in our way. We think He isn't leading us in the right direction or fast enough. We think God isn't leading us at all. Freedom to go our own way steals our humility and we take God's control.

When trouble blocks your path and makes you question God's leadership, read the book of Exodus. It is a great example of how we humans lose our way on life's path when we don't rely on God's GPS! Recognize that God has control. He is always a step ahead of you and ready to save you from whatever enslaves you in this mixed-up human world. If you allow God to lead, you will find freedom and true joy knowing that your destination is in His sight.

Thou wilt shew me the path of life: in thy presence is fulness of joy; at thy right hand there are pleasures for evermore.
PSALM 16:11

The Blank Page

When the Israelites thought God abandoned them on a road to nowhere, they lost their trust in Him. Their joy turned to despair and anger. Don't let that happen to you! When you feel uncertain about which way to go, there are methods to get on the right path.

- Seek God's will for you by praying and meditating on His Word.
- Trust Him to show you the way.
- Practice patience.
- Hold on to optimism. "'For I know the plans I have for you,' declares the LORD, 'plans to prosper you and not to harm you, plans to give you hope and a future'" (Jeremiah 29:11 NIV).
- Stay humble.
- Believe that God has everything under control.
- Know that His plans for you are good.
- If He leads you outside your comfort zone, don't be afraid.
- If He seems far away, trust that He has not abandoned you. God is ahead of you, leading your way.
- Remember, God will reveal His plan for you one step at a time. He sees the big picture. He knows where you are going and the best way to get there.

The Last Word

When God created humans, He allowed them freedom to choose whether to obey Him. The first example of this God-given right to freedom is found in Genesis 2:16–17 (NIV): God tells Adam, "You are free to eat from any tree in the garden; but you must not eat from the tree of the knowledge of good and evil, for when you eat from it you will certainly die." Adam and his partner, Eve, had complete freedom to choose except for one simple rule—and they broke it! That one act of defiance, eating from the forbidden tree, unleashed sin into the world. If God hadn't sent Jesus to save us from sin, we might still be enslaved to it.

God continues to give us freedom to choose. There is joy in that! Even greater joy comes with knowing God won't abandon us when we make wrong choices. Our greatest joy is found in His consistent forgiveness, presence, and love. "God loved the people of this world so much that he gave his only Son, so that everyone who has faith in him will have eternal life and never really die" (John 3:16 CEV). God's love and desire to be present with us has no end.

Think about the choices you make. Are they pleasing to God? You can study your Bible to learn the kinds of behavior He expects from you. Then honor Him by choosing to obey.

Week 1: DAY SEVEN

PUTTING IT ALL TOGETHER

C. S. Lewis said, "Progress means getting nearer to the place you want to be. And if you have taken a wrong turning, then to go forward does not get you any nearer. If you are on the wrong road, progress means doing an about-turn and walking back to the right road; and in that case the [one] who turns back soonest is the most progressive [one]."[1]

Week one began with this question: Where are you on your path through life? After reading this week's devotionals and applying them, would you answer differently now?

If you think you are on the wrong path or if you feel lost, you might say, "I don't know what to do," or "I don't know which way to go." It makes sense then to stop and turn on God's GPS. Believe that He can do anything. Let Him take the lead, and give Him control. Allow God to guide you back in the right direction.

Your role is to follow Him, have faith in Him, and remember to connect your faith with trust. Be persistent in prayer asking for His help. Be brave. Go where He leads you. And have patience when God asks you to wait.

With each small step, the way back will become more familiar. Praise God! Thank Him for loving you and staying with you. The

[1] C. S. Lewis, *Mere Christianity*, in *The Complete C. S. Lewis* (San Francisco: HarperSanFrancisco, 2002), 33.

road back is never lonely if you remember that He is ever present. At a crossroad He gives you freedom to choose. Ask Him to help you make the best choice according to His will. If you do these things, God will lead you back to the path He has made for you.

God is joy—true, complete joy. He is not a feeling. He lives in your heart, existing as one with you, loving you always, going everywhere with you, guiding you and keeping you safe. God is the source of all joy. Even when your road is rough, there is joy because He is with you and in you. When you put all your belief and trust in Him, you have confidence to overcome obstacles in your way. When the Lord guides you through and beyond a road-block, you can look back and say, "I did that!": "I can do all things through Christ who strengthens me" (Philippians 4:13 NKJV).

Try to radiate joy wherever you go—it is one of the best ways to lead others to discover true joy in Jesus. Smile, even when you don't feel like it. Be encouraging, not only to others but also to yourself.

Finally, savor all the little joys, the blessings, you discover along the way. Don't run. Walk. Otherwise you might miss them. There is joy on life's path from beginning to end. "Rejoice always" (1 Thessalonians 5:16 NIV) is one of the shortest verses in the bible and so easy to remember. Every day, every minute of your life, REJOICE!

Thou wilt shew me the path of life: in thy presence is fulness of joy; at thy right hand there are pleasures for evermore.

PSALM 16:11

The Blank Page

Meditating on God's words in the Bible makes you aware of how much He loves you and also grows your love for Him. Have you memorized this week's Bible verse? Memorizing scripture is important because it provides you with a deeper understanding of God and His will. Knowing what God expects from you can lead to obedience when you face temptations. Building a tower of memorized scripture equips you for any situation you might face. His words help you to be brave; they comfort, motivate, challenge, heal, and provide peace and stability. If you believe memorizing scripture is too hard or unnecessary, do it anyway. Write His words on your heart so they are with you wherever you go.

God wants you to memorize and share His words. Deuteronomy 6:6–7 (CEV) says, "Memorize his laws and tell them to your children over and over again. Talk about them all the time, whether you're at home or walking along the road or going to bed at night, or getting up in the morning."

Use the index cards in this book to help you. Write the words until you have them memorized. Record them. Use the other memory tips you've learned this week or your own. There is no wrong way to go about it.

The author of Psalm 119 wrote, "[God,] Your word is a lamp to my feet and a light to my path" (v. 105 NKJV). Keep God's words in your heart, and allow them to light your way.

The Last Word

Dear God, thank You for traveling life with me. It brings me joy knowing that You are with me, always in my heart. When I stray from my path, guide me back. Keep me from temptations, and lead me away from the enemy's traps. When obstacles get in my way, make me strong. Help me to be brave and not turn back. God, I trust You. I will remember that You are my Shepherd, the One who loves and cares for me. I know I am safe with You wherever I go. "Thou wilt shew me the path of life: in thy presence is fulness of joy; at thy right hand there are pleasures for evermore." Amen.

Week 2

FINDING JOY IN GOD'S CREATIONS

This is the day which the Lord hath made; we will rejoice and be glad in it.

Psalm 118:24

A QUIET, GENTLE SPIRIT

You are amazing. Not just because of who you are, but because of what you are—a soul, a life, one with God and set inside an incredible machine, a human body created by Him.

David wrote in Psalm 139:14 (NKJV): "I will praise You, for I am fearfully and wonderfully made; marvelous are Your works, and that my soul knows very well." Think about you as God's creation. Inside your framework of bones is an intricate system, a factory made up of organs operating together, keeping your body working and alive. A mix of chemicals is added so the food you eat creates fuel giving you power for work and play. God even built in safety measures to keep your body at the right temperature and a repair system to heal broken parts. Your brain, the control center, allows you to move. It activates your senses, giving you the ability to see, hear, taste, smell, and feel whatever you touch. Think about that. If it weren't for your senses, you would be a soul, a life, trapped inside a body. God made you able to see, hear, taste, smell, and touch so you have access to everything He created here on earth and even into the sky. Isn't that reason to praise Him?

This week we will explore finding joy in God's creations, beginning with you. Look in the mirror. How would you describe yourself to someone who couldn't see you? What adjectives would you use to describe your physical appearance?

First Peter 3:3-4 (NKJV) says: "Do not let your adornment be merely outward—arranging the hair, wearing gold, or putting on fine apparel—rather let it be the hidden person of the heart, with the incorruptible beauty of a gentle and quiet spirit, which is very precious in the sight of God." Notice the word *merely*. It isn't wrong to look nice. But true beauty comes from your soul connection with the Creator. When you work toward having a gentle and quiet spirit, God sees your incorruptible—constant—beauty. You are precious in His sight. Even on bad hair days and days without any makeup God thinks you are beautiful!

A quiet spirit is one that is not too busy to see beauty in the world. It is a gentle spirit that not only sees but appreciates God's goodness every day. You radiate true beauty when you find joy in yourself. It begins with you! Unless you first find joy in who you are—God's creation and His beloved child—your senses can't fully enjoy and rejoice over all the wonderful blessings He puts around you.

There are so many things about you that are beautiful: the way you love, your caring and kindness, the times you put the needs of others ahead of your own. . . . There is a quiet and gentle spirit within you. God sees it, and He wants you to see it too.

This is the day which the LORD hath made;
we will rejoice and be glad in it.
PSALM 118:24

The Blank Page

Discovering your inner beauty starts when you connect with your Creator. Begin each day talking with God. Ask Him to help you block any negative self-talk, and ask Him to show you the beauty He set within you.

Recognize your worth as the daughter of the King of all kings, the Creator of the universe. Throughout the day, notice your words and actions. Make a list of all that are good: when you smile or share laughter with someone, how you listen attentively with concern, the things you say and do to be kind and helpful. Keep in mind the idea of a quiet and gentle spirit—one that isn't too wrapped up in itself or the world to see and appreciate God's blessings. At the end of the day, tell God about the beauty you found inside you, and thank Him for putting it there.

You might decide you need to work on your inner beauty. Could it be you are too hard on yourself or expecting too much? Self-deprecation is the enemy's way of stealing your beauty, your God-given worth. Don't allow it to happen! Turn your thoughts to God's love for you. As His love grows within you, so will your love for yourself.

God made you. He gave you everything you need to open yourself to the beauty within and around you. God made this day, and He gave you life today. So live it joyfully. Allow your beautiful self to shine!

The Last Word

You know what it's like to get a song stuck in your head. It plays over and over, bridging your thoughts. Even at night when you snuggle quiet in your bed, there's that song. "It's so annoying!" you say. "I hate when that happens!" But what if that song were a Bible verse playing endlessly in your thoughts? Surely you would commit it to memory and—bonus—that verse added to the others you memorized would become a part of you, the way you think and act.

Try this. Make up a melody and sing the words of this week's memory verse: *"This is the day which the LORD hath made; we will rejoice and be glad in it."*

Sing it again and again until you can't get it out of your head! Sing it out loud at home until your family members can't get it out of their heads!

Paul says, in 2 Timothy 3:16–17 (NIV), "All Scripture is God-breathed and is useful for teaching, rebuking, correcting and training in righteousness, so that the servant of God may be thoroughly equipped for every good work." Memorizing scripture verses and putting them into action is key to how you react to every situation. If you are teaching, rebuking, correcting, training, or just spending time with family or friends, you will glow with inner beauty if you know God's Word and put it to use.

Week 2: DAY TWO

LiTTLE THiNGS

The British novelist Barbara Pym found joy in anthropology. Tiny uncovered treasures led her to create characters who valued little blessings. In her novel *Less Than Angels*, Pym's main character, Catherine Oliphant, observes: "The small things of life were often so much bigger than the great things. . .the trivial pleasures like cooking, one's home, little poems. . .solitary walks, funny things seen and overheard."[2]

How often we forget to rejoice in trivial pleasures! The smell of the earth in springtime. The intricate shape of a single snowflake landing on a mitten. The refreshing way ice-cold water feels going down when you've worked in the garden in the hot summer sun. Little things. Mundane things. Wonderful small things that God provides us every day.

The world is filled with tiny treasures if only we open our senses. *The Guinness Book of World Records* has a plethora of information about little things. For example, if you live in Cuba, you might see the world's smallest bird—the bee hummingbird, 2.24 inches long. If you live in Portland, Oregon, you probably know of Mill Ends Park, the smallest park in the world—just 24 inches round, it sits on a safety island on SW Front Avenue. If you open your eyes to the little things, God will reveal them

[2] Barbara Pym, *Less Than Angels*, first edition (E.P. Dutton, 1980).

to you, although maybe not with the same keen eyesight He provided young Veronica Seider, a student at the University of Stuttgart in Germany in 1972. According to *Guinness*, her eyesight was twenty times greater than average, and she could identify people at a distance of more than a mile!

Little things open our eyes to big things. Jesus compared the mustard seed, one of the smallest seeds on earth, to the kingdom of God. He said, "Though it is the smallest of all seeds, yet when it grows, it is the largest of garden plants and becomes a tree, so that the birds come and perch in its branches" (Matthew 13:32 NIV).

Luke 10:38–42 tells the story of sisters Mary and Martha, friends of Jesus. They opened their home to Him and His disciples. While Martha was busy multitasking, trying to be a perfect host, she became irritated with Mary, who did just one small thing—sit and listen to Jesus' wise words. But Jesus said, "Martha, Martha. . .you are worried and upset about many things, but few things are needed—or indeed only one. Mary, has chosen what is better, and it will not be taken away from her" (vv. 41–42 NIV).

The Lord is all around you in the tiniest things. His wisdom is hidden in them. Through little things He will teach you bigger things, wonderful things, joyful things!—if you stop long enough to notice.

Zechariah 4:10 (NCV) reminds us: "The people should not think that small beginnings are unimportant." Every big idea begins with a tiny observation. So unleash your senses. Discover what God wants to show you today.

This is the day which the LORD hath made;
we will rejoice and be glad in it.
PSALM 118:24

The Blank Page

There is a modern proverb: *God is in the detail*. Remember those five words today. Your task is to break down big things into their smallest parts.

Ask God to open all your senses. Take a walk around your neighborhood or workplace. Walk slowly, soaking up your surroundings, opening yourself to the tiniest things. Observe how people relate to one another, the little things they say or do and the impact it has on their relationships. Listen closely. What do you hear beyond all the noise? Become aware of faint smells. Taste something new today, something outside your comfort zone, just one tiny taste. Study nature. Look up. Look down. Notice the weather, how even a quick rain shower or sudden burst of snow changes the earth. Learn about God's faithfulness by watching birds and wildlife. See how He provides their every need.

Along the way, thank God for all the little things you discover.

> *Sing to the LORD with thanksgiving;*
> *Sing praises. . .to our God,*
> *Who covers the heavens with clouds,*
> *Who prepares rain for the earth,*
> *Who makes grass to grow on the mountains.*
> *He gives to the beast its food,*
> *And to the young ravens that cry.*
> PSALM 147:7–9 NKJV

Praise Him today for revealing to you His many hidden treasures. Tonight, reflect on the little things that brought you the greatest joy.

The Last Word

Jesus' death on the cross changed the world. Since the time of His crucifixion and resurrection, Christianity has become the leading world religion. Today there are more than 2.5 billion Christians in the world.

It all seems very big, doesn't it—His death, resurrection, the growth of Christianity? But to become a follower of Jesus and be saved, it takes just one little act: accepting Jesus as your Lord and Savior. "If you declare with your mouth, 'Jesus is Lord,' and if you believe in your heart that God raised Jesus from the dead, you will be saved" (Romans 10:9 NCV). That small act of faith is not only your ticket to forever life in heaven, but also a seed planted in your heart. Like the tiny mustard seed, it grows. Great ministries and businesses have sprung up from that tiny seed growing in the heart of a woman or a man. Think about that.

Every day you can find joy in having completed that one small act of accepting Jesus into your heart. Then you can trust God to turn it into something big. Robert Schuller said, "Anyone can count the seeds in an apple, but only God can count the number of apples in a seed." Ask God today to grow your faith and lead you toward His purpose for you. Don't dismiss any little ideas. Remember, it was a small stone David used to kill Goliath and a little boy's lunch that fed five thousand.

"The heavens declare the glory of God, and the skies announce what his hands have made" (Psalm 19:1 NCV). The sky is ever changing. Clear blue with soft white clouds—it gives way to thunderclouds and pouring rain. A fiery sunset follows the rainbow. A slow fade to gray then darkness. The moon. Distant planets. An endless sea of stars. . .

Gordon Cooper, one of America's first astronauts, prayed while in a space capsule orbiting Earth. He said, "Father, thank You, especially for letting me fly this flight. . .for the privilege of being able to be in this position, to be in this wondrous place, seeing all these many startling, wonderful things that You have created." Cooper, who until then had been looking up from earth, now saw the sky with a new perspective, and what he saw was unlike anything he had ever seen.

Look up.

God told Abram to look up. He said, "Look up at the sky and count the stars—if indeed you can count them" (Genesis 15:5 NIV). Psalm 147:4 tells us God determines the number of stars, and He calls each one by name. God is so magnificent that even the sun, moon, and stars praise Him (see Psalm 148:3)! The book of Job says that while God was creating the earth "the morning stars sang together and all the angels shouted for joy" (Job 38:7 NIV).

Do you feel joy when you look up at God's stars?

In *The Little Prince*, by Antoine de Saint-Exupéry, the prince says, "All men have stars, but they are not the same things for different people. For some, who are travelers, the stars are guides. For others they are no more than little lights in the sky. For others, who are scholars, they are problems. . . . But all these stars are silent. You—You alone will have stars as no one else has them."[3]

How do *you* see the stars? One person looks up and finds joy in them. Another sees little lights or nothing. Some are so busy analyzing the stars that they forget that stars have a Creator.

"Look up." Think about those words and what they mean. Taken literally, they command you to lift your head and see something. Figuratively they invite you to look beyond what is seen and discover something even better: "Things are looking up!"

Every day God allows you to choose whether to look up—or not. But looking up, either literally or figuratively, can change how you perceive your day and life. If you literally look up, you can admire the handiwork of the One who holds the stars. If you look beyond, you will discover the One who holds you in the palm of His hand. You are part of His great creation, the universe beyond the sky. If you remember that and find joy in His presence, then every day will be a good one.

This is the day which the LORD hath made;
we will rejoice and be glad in it.
PSALM 118:24

[3] Antoine de Saint-Exupéry, *The Little Prince*, gift edition (Houghton Mifflin Harcourt, 2015), 94.

The Blank Page

WHEN I HEARD THE LEARN'D ASTRONOMER
Walt Whitman

When I heard the learn'd astronomer,
When the proofs, the figures, were ranged in columns
 before me,
When I was shown the charts and diagrams, to add,
 divide, and measure them,
When I sitting heard the astronomer where he
 lectured with much applause in the lecture-room,
How soon unaccountable I became tired and sick,
Till rising and gliding out I wander'd off by myself,
In the mystical moist night-air, and from time to time,
Look'd up in perfect silence at the stars.

Most days are cluttered with facts and figures, not unlike the astronomer's lecture in Walt Whitman's poem. Cluttered with obligations, meetings, chores… Sometimes, like the narrator in the poem, we feel tired and sick of it all. We need to get away.

Take a few minutes today and "glide out." Wander off by yourself somewhere silent. Look up toward the stars, toward heaven and God, your Creator. Pray. Listen for His voice. Soak up His words. Then like the sun, moon, and stars, praise Him! Like the angels, shout for joy (if only in your heart). This is the day which the Lord has made! For that, rejoice and be glad.

The Last Word

You can see many things in the sky with your naked eyes. In daytime, clouds, the sun, a rainbow. At night, the moon, stars, satellites, planets closest to Earth. If you look closer, you will see constellations. If you watch the sky long enough, you might see a meteor or even a meteor shower. You could see the International Space Station moving quickly through the darkness like a big, white dot. If you used a telescope, you would see even more of the sky. But the most powerful telescopes can't see all of it. Humans keep searching, venturing farther into space trying to uncover its secrets. What is beyond the stars?

Thousands of years ago, Job's friend Zophar asked, "Can you fathom the mysteries of God? Can you probe the limits of the Almighty? They are higher than the heavens above" (Job 11:7–8 NIV).

Do you wonder why God is sometimes secretive, hiding things from us—things only He can know? Do you wonder what is beyond the stars?

Maybe God hides things from us because He wants us to seek Him. In doing so, we grow closer to Him. We learn to trust Him with what we cannot see and with all the days of our lives.

Look up! Believe that God is there. Don't be afraid to step into the unknown. God knows who you are, and He loves you. He knows what is ahead of you, and He will guide you there.

God's oceans and seas are some of the most beautiful settings on earth. Who doesn't find joy walking barefoot on a beach or sitting in the sand with a loved one watching the sun rise or set? But the sea has an angry side. The power of its waves is beyond human control. Only God can hold it back. He did it for the Israelites when He parted the Red Sea so they could cross. He saved Jonah when he was thrown overboard and swallowed by a big fish. God rescued the apostle Paul from several shipwrecks. One can only guess how many people have been saved by God's grace from a devilish sea.

John Newton, born in 1725, was the son of a ship captain. At age eleven, wanting nothing to do with his father and stepmother, John left home and went to sea. In the company of rough sailors, he rejected his mother's Christian teaching and her prayers pleading with God to make her son a minister. John grew into an immoral young man known as "the great blasphemer." He even tried to rob others of their belief in God, and succeeded.

He was aboard a ship, the *Greyhound*, in 1748 when a great storm hit, rocking the wooden ship and threatening to break it apart. As water washed over the deck swallowing some of John's shipmates, he worked furiously pumping water, trying to keep the ship afloat. "God, have mercy!" John shouted. He continued praying while taking the helm. Then, after many hours, the winds died down. The *Greyhound* drifted to an island, arriving just as the last of the crew's food and water ran out. John Newton's life had been ever changed by God's grace.

The prayers of his mother were answered. John became a minister, an energetic evangelist. He began writing hymns for his services. One of them, inspired by his conversion during the terrible storm in the North Atlantic, remains popular today:

"Amazing Grace! How sweet the sound
That saved a wretch like me!
I once was lost, but now am found;
Was blind but now I see...."

God created your life. He wants you to live it joyfully and abundantly. When life's ocean gets rough, if you worry you'll drown in your trouble, the devil will take that, and like what happened to John Newton, he will try to steal your faith. But in the worst of storms remember—God is there. He will rescue you when you ask for His mercy. His grace is present today and every day. His grace is amazing, indeed!

"Through many dangers, toils, and snares,
I have already come;
'Tis grace hath brought me safe thus far,
And grace will lead me home.
The Lord has promised good to me,
His Word my hope secures;
He will my Shield and Portion be,
As long as life endures."

This is the day which the LORD hath made;
we will rejoice and be glad in it.
PSALM 118:24

The Blank Page

Humans explore the depths of the oceans and climb to the peaks of the highest mountains to experience the beauty of God's creations. The force at those depths and heights is sometimes more than a human can endure. Sometimes God has to rescue His children when they climb too high or sink too low. This is true literally and also in life. We need God, our Rescuer. We all have times when, like John Newton, we cry out, "God, have mercy!"

Today, think about times when God has rescued you. It doesn't have to be anything big. He rescues often in small ways, like reminding you to look up from your cell phone before you step off a curb or to look down so you don't slip on a patch of ice. God rescues you from yourself too. Think about times when you might have made a mistake but didn't because He intervened and led you in a better direction, or when you felt down and He found a way to lift your spirits. And finally, meditate today on God's greatest rescue, saving you from sin through His Son, Jesus. Galatians 1:4–5 (CEV) says: "Christ obeyed God our Father and gave himself as a sacrifice for our sins to rescue us from this evil world. God will be given glory forever and ever. Amen."

The Last Word

We live in an age where technology helps with almost everything! Your computer, tablet, or smartphone might be one of the best tools for helping you to memorize scripture.

This is the day which the LORD hath made;
we will rejoice and be glad in it.

PSALM 118:24

Have you memorized this week's verse? Here are five ways technology can help.

1. Use a digital voice assistant, like Alexa or Siri, to remind you. "_____, remind me in an hour to recite today's verse." Reset the reminder for every hour until you've committed the verse to memory. Or simply set an alarm on your smartphone.

2. Email the verse to yourself or work with a buddy and text the verse to each other.

3. Use your smartphone's recording technology to record the verse, then listen to it often and repeat it.

4. Take a picture of this week's scripture memory card. Make it the screen saver on your smartphone.

5. There's an app for that! Search for Bible memory apps that can help with memorization. There are many to choose from. Find one you like, and use it.

Think of other ways you could use your computer, tablet, or phone as a help for memorizing scripture. God the Creator gave you special skills and talents. How might you combine them with technology to create a scripture memory tool?

BLESS THE BEASTS

Genesis 2 tells about the seventh day of creation when God placed Adam in the garden of Eden. Even before God created Eve as a partner for Adam, He made animals to keep Adam company. He brought them to Adam and allowed him to name each one. Does that sound familiar? Every day, God brings animals to humans and vice versa. Humans adopt animals as pets, name them, and accept them as companions.

Second Samuel 12 shares a story that proves as long ago as the tenth century BC humans had pets and treated them much the same as we do our pets today. God sent the prophet Nathan to David with a parable that said in part, "The poor man had only one little lamb that he had bought and raised. The lamb became a pet for him and his children. He even let it eat from his plate and drink from his cup and sleep on his lap. The lamb was like one of his own children" (v. 3 CEV).

Pets play an important role as our companions. They bring us joy. But God also uses them as His helpers.

On September 11, 2001, the day two commercial airliners crashed into both towers of the World Trade Center in New York City, Michael Hingson was at work on the 78th floor of the North Tower. His guide dog, Roselle, was at his side. God had brought

Michael and Roselle together in 1999. Michael, blind since birth, had received his first guide dog at age fourteen. There had been four others before Roselle. God gave each one a purpose helping to lead Michael through specific phases of his life.

At 8:26 a.m. on September 11, Michael and Roselle heard a huge explosion and felt the North Tower sway. "God, don't let this tower fall," Michael prayed. Roselle moved closer to him, calm but ready. In the lead, sensing danger, she guided Michael down seventy-eight floors, more than 1,400 stairs. It took an hour. As they exited the building, the South Tower started to fall. Michael heard and knew what was happening. His first instinct was to ask God why. But at the same time, God was telling Michael to trust Roselle. She ran with Michael hanging on tight to her lead. Through a giant dust cloud with small bits of debris raining down on them, Roselle led Michael to safety.

Each day, God gives His animals in service to assist people with disabilities and in law enforcement. But most of all, He uses animals to bring us joy and teach us more about Him. Job 12:7–10 (NIV) says: "But ask the animals, and they will teach you, or the birds in the sky, and they will tell you. . .or let the fish in the sea inform you. Which of all these does not know that [in] the hand of the LORD. . .is the life of every creature and the breath of all mankind."

This is the day which the LORD hath made;
we will rejoice and be glad in it.
PSALM 118:24

The Blank Page

Frances Hodgson Burnett wrote these thought-provoking words in her novel *A Little Princess*: "How it is that animals understand things I do not know, but it is certain that they do understand. Perhaps there is a language which is not made of words and everything in the world understands it. Perhaps there is a soul hidden in everything and it can always speak, without even making a sound, to another soul."

Your challenge today is to observe animals, your own pets or the wild birds and other creatures where you live. See what they have to teach you about life. Watch for examples of

Forgiveness

Determination

Patience

Faithfulness

Responsibility

Goals

Listening

Teamwork

Trust

Rest

Play

Love. . .and, of course,

Joy!

Open your eyes to God's animals. Watch closely, and He will use them to inspire and teach you.

The Last Word

The Bible has many examples of God using animals as His helpers. In the story of Noah and the flood, God used a dove to show Noah that the waters had receded from the earth. He used a talking donkey to convict Balaam, a wayward prophet, of his sins. And when Jonah was thrown into a stormy sea, God used a big fish, not only to rescue Jonah from drowning but also to get Jonah to a place where he listened to God and obeyed His instructions, which in turn saved the city of Nineveh.

In the Bible we also find the analogy of Him as our Shepherd and we as His sheep. Jesus said He came to save the lost sheep, those who had no shepherd. When we accept Christ as our Shepherd, He cares for us! If we get lost, Jesus promises to find us. He provides for us as a shepherd provides for his sheep. The Bible also says that as His sheep, we come to know Jesus' voice. We learn to trust Him to lead us. Jesus goes before us, and we follow Him (see John 10:2–4). The apostle Peter referred to Jesus as the "Shepherd and Overseer" of our souls (1 Peter 2:25 NIV). Jesus told Peter, "Feed My sheep"—share the truth about Him with others.

Think about it: What is your relationship with the Shepherd? Have you fed His "sheep" today?

"In the beginning God created the heaven and the earth." These first words of the Bible continue, revealing that God created night and day; sky and land; plants; the sun, moon, stars; animals; and humans. These are the things we most often think of when we ponder God's creation. But they are only the beginning of His creation story.

When God created man, the Bible says He created him in His own image (see Genesis 1:27). In many ways, we are like God, a shadow of Him. When we come to know Him through His Word, we learn what He expects from us: to act as His representatives on earth, living as best we can in His image as the Creator of all things good.

We can also think of ourselves as God's helpers stretching out His creation story through time. Think about this. God set within us the desire and ability to create. Music, art, words made into stories. . .the list of what women and men have created and continue to create is endless. Through this God-given ability we are like our Creator. It is Him working through us. A good example of this is Exodus 35:10–35 in which God uses the skills and talents of His people to build a tabernacle, a beautiful place where He would dwell among the people of Israel. Take a few minutes to read in your Bible about the diversity of creative skills His people had and used.

What we create doesn't need to be a great work of art, a bestselling novel, or the most beautiful song ever heard. Whatever we create, even something insignificant, it should bring us joy. And when we share our creations with others, it can bring them joy too. But as creators we need to be careful. If God gave us the talent to create, then He also cares about what we create. In Genesis, after God made something, He surveyed what He had done and announced that it was good. He expects our creations to be good too! Not necessarily aesthetically good, but good in ways that honor Him. God gives us freedom to choose what we create. Our words, images, and ideas should be free of anything that would not make Him proud to see and proclaim that one of His children made it—*and it was good.*

Do your creations bring you joy? Did the birthday cake you baked result in some smiles? "Oooo, it's so pretty!" "Oh, this tastes good!" That was God the Creator working through you, not only bringing joy to you but also spreading some joy around. Did words you wrote in a card touch someone's heart and make that person feel loved? That was God the Creator working through you too. Whatever you do that is creative, no matter how small, remember you are God's helper. You are continuing His creation story, helping Him to make today and every day good.

This is the day which the Lord hath made;
we will rejoice and be glad in it.
PSALM 118:24

The Blank Page

Look around your house or workplace. Most of what you see was created by human minds and hands. An idea grew into something solid, something meant to be shared, something built to make life easier or bring someone joy.

Your task today is to create one thing to share with someone. Maybe you feel like skipping this because your schedule is already full. But remember—a creation doesn't have to be big or time-consuming. Write a sweet little love note to pack with your husband's lunch. Tell your child a story, one you make up. Create a fun little game to play with your family at dinnertime.

If you have more time to spend, put extra effort into dinner by setting a pretty table and making something special and a little out of the ordinary for a weekday meal. Or you could bake something and give it to a neighbor or make a little gift for a friend.

Finally, take an inventory of your talents and skills. Plan to share at least one in a bigger way in the future. Think about how you can use your gift to enrich your church, your community, or even the world. Mother Teresa said, "It's not how much we give, but how much love we put into giving." Whatever talent you decide to share, share it with love, and do it joyfully. Do it in the image of God.

The Last Word

George Washington Carver is someone who asked God questions. When God answered, ideas were born, and Carver acted on those ideas to create something good. In his own words, he described how a prayer inspired him to use a simple thing like peanuts in unique ways:

" 'Dear Mr. Creator, please tell me what the universe was made for.' The Great Creator answered, 'You want to know too much for that little mind of yours. Ask for something more your size.' Then I asked, 'Dear Mr. Creator tell me what man was made for.' Again, the Great Creator replied, 'Little man, you are still asking too much. Cut down the extent of your request and improve the intent.' So, then I asked, 'Please Mr. Creator will you tell me why the peanut was made?' "

Slowly, God revealed His ideas to Carver, and with them Carver created peanut products, not only food products but also cosmetics, fuels, paints, and even insecticides. Always, Carver gave God the credit. "I never have to grope for methods," he said. "The method is revealed at the moment I am inspired to create something new. . . . Without God to draw aside the curtain I would be helpless."[4]

What a magnificent example of God working through one of His children to create something good!

Do you have questions for God? Ask! He might have a great idea ready and waiting for you.

---

[4] William J. Federer, *America's God and Country Encyclopedia of Quotations*, revised edition (Amerisearch: 2000), 95.

You are God's creation, and He made you to be His partner. Together you and God can make the world a better place through the skills and talents He set within you. Your job is to open yourself to Him and learn. Ask God questions, like George Washington Carver did. Use your senses to explore everything around you expecting God to reveal Himself to you. God says, "Be still, and know that I am God" (Psalm 46:10). So quiet your spirit. Be gentle. Look for Him in the smallest of things. Look up as far as you can into the sky and wonder about what you cannot see. Watch what animals do. Remember God works through them too, helping you learn. Find joy in the life God gave you. When trouble comes, believe His grace will save you.

Observing God's creations and learning from them is only the beginning. Next, you need to apply what you've learned. Pray and ask God to show you how you can combine your skills and talents with what He wants you to do. Believe that He has a plan. God gave you things you are good at for a reason, to serve Him in some way. Ask Him to lead you.

First Peter 4:10 (NIV) says, "Each of you should use whatever gift you have received to serve others, as faithful stewards of God's grace in its various forms." Use your skills and talents to bless others. Are you good at making crafts? Volunteer to teach a class at your church or a community center. Do you like to sing or play a musical instrument? A nursing home would love to have you come and entertain their residents by leading a sing-along or playing live music. If you are a good cook or baker, start a group at your church; partner with others to provide meals for those in your congregation who are recovering from surgery or busy caring for a loved one. Plant a vegetable garden and share what you grow. Coach sports. Create fun games and activities to do with kids. If you enjoy working with numbers, help others prepare their taxes. There are endless ways to bless others through your own God-given talents and skills.

When you share what you are good at, you are helping to build God's kingdom. Think of it as a ministry. Remember that you were made in His image, and do your best to be like Him. Always be open to telling others that God is the One who leads you to create good things. Give Him the credit for your success.

On this day, the day that the Lord has made, rejoice and be glad that you are His creation. Be glad that He gave you life and an abundance of wonderful things to discover. Be glad for His gifts of your skills and talents. And also be glad for the gifts of others that bring joy to you!

This is the day which the Lord hath made;
we will rejoice and be glad in it.
PSALM 118:24

The Blank Page

God made your brain to create and hold memories. Think of it as your computer. Some memories are readily available on your desktop. Other files you need to search for. Some pop up unexpectedly. "Oh, now I remember that file!"

Once you memorize a scripture verse, it's in there! You made a choice about where to store it. You either put it on your desktop for easy recall, filed it away, or maybe you even forgot about it.

Get in the habit of storing scripture front and center in your brain. Open those files often, and apply them to your daily life. Add to them. Organize scripture in your mind by themes so when you face a specific situation you can open a folder and find everything you need. Keep in mind that Satan is like a computer virus. It brings him joy to destroy your files. Don't let him! Be vigilant. Protect your brain with scripture verses that will stop him better than the best virus protection software.

Romans 12:2 (CEV) says, "Don't be like the people of this world, but let God change the way you think. Then you will know how to do everything that is good and pleasing to him." Pray and ask God to help you change the way you think. Make His words the first files you open every day.

The Last Word

Dear God, this is the day You have made. I will rejoice and be glad in it! Thank You for opening my senses to the wonders of Your creation. Help me to have a quiet, gentle spirit so I will notice and learn from the little blessings You place all around me. You've given me so many reasons to be joyful. Forgive me for days when I don't feel joy. Even then, Your grace is there to lift me up. I am grateful for the skills and talents You have given me. Show me how to use them to bring happiness to others. You created me in Your image, Father. Lead me always to be a reflection of Your goodness and love. Amen.

Week 3
FINDING JOY IN YOUR RELATIONSHIPS

And be ye kind one to another, tenderhearted, forgiving one another, even as God for Christ's sake hath forgiven you.

EPHESIANS 4:32

Week 3: DAY ONE

GOD, MY FATHER

Bookstore shelves overflow with self-help books about relationships. But there is one book that leads them all. It is the most read book in the world. It has sold more than any other book in history. That book is the Bible. The Bible's first two chapters begin the true story of our relationship with God. He is the Father of us all. We are His children, and the relationship we form with Him is key to every other relationship we have.

When God created humans, He gave us space to be ourselves and grow. He allowed us freedom to choose. He set rules for us, good rules to protect us and guide us through life. The first humans, Adam and Eve, had just one rule: "You may eat fruit from any tree in the garden, except the one that has the power to let you know the difference between right and wrong" (Genesis 2:16–17 CEV). Like all children, Adam and Eve used their free will to break their Father's rule. There were consequences. God disciplined them. But He didn't take away their freedom to choose between right and wrong. He kept on trying to teach His children, wanting them to see that His advice was perfect. It would save them from a lifetime of trouble if only they chose to trust and obey Him.

Throughout the Bible, God has advice for every kind of relationship. He wants us to learn from Him how to live peacefully with our marriage partners, children, parents, siblings, friends, coworkers, strangers, and even those who hate us. His advice is all there in the Bible for us to read, learn, and put into practice. But even more important than His words is the relationship we have with Him.

God, our Father, is present with us always. He is never too busy to listen and provide guidance. He disciplines out of love with the purpose of setting us on the right path. He readily forgives. God never misses important events in our lives. He is there for every birthday, graduation, wedding, and funeral. He celebrates our achievements and comforts us in trouble. His love is pure, unconditional, and never ending. The way God relates to us is consistent. He says, "I am the LORD All-Powerful, and I never change" (Malachi 3:6 CEV).

Forming a strong bond with our heavenly Father and following His advice is the key to good human relationships. The closer we get to God, the more we allow Him to guide us. When we listen to and follow His advice, then we become better people. When we become better, our relationships with others get better. The Scottish evangelist Henry Drummond wrote: "There are some men and some women in whose company we are always at our best. While with them we cannot think mean thoughts or speak ungenerous words." This week, we will explore how a good relationship with God can lead you to become that kind of person.

And be ye kind one to another, tenderhearted, forgiving one another, even as God for Christ's sake hath forgiven you.
Ephesians 4:32

The Blank Page

Compare your relationship with God five years ago to the relationship you have with Him today. Here are ten questions to guide your thinking:

1. Overall, have you grown closer with God?
2. Has your relationship with your heavenly Father made you a better person?
3. Have you dug deeper into Bible study?
4. Do you spend more time now praying and listening to Him?
5. Has your trust in Him grown?
6. Are you more aware of what God expects from you?
7. Have you become more compliant with His rules?
8. Are you more comfortable sharing your faith with others?
9. Do you think about God more often throughout the day?
10. Do you rely more on Him for guiding your decisions?

If your bond with God hasn't grown stronger during the last five years, think of ways you can improve it. Prayer is the best starting point. Talk with God about how you plan to make a more powerful connection with Him. If your relationship doesn't feel stronger right away, persevere. Believe that God is drawing you nearer to Him. Trust in His love. Relationships are ever changing, and this is true of your relationship with God. Every relationship has its ups and downs. If you go through a down time with God, don't panic. He is not going to be angry or leave you. Your heavenly Father is waiting with open arms to welcome you home.

The Last Word

Longer scripture verses can be more difficult to memorize. Our minds sometimes want to change the order of the words, insert words that are not there, and even delete words. One way to avoid this is to break the verse into easy-to-remember parts.

1. Memorize the scripture reference. Say it often—"Ephesians 4:32."
2. After you have memorized the reference, find Ephesians 4:32 in your Bible and read it aloud: "And be ye kind one to another, tenderhearted, forgiving one another, even as God for Christ's sake hath forgiven you."
3. Decide how you can break the passage into memory parts:

    And be ye kind one to another,
    tenderhearted, forgiving one another,
    even as God for Christ's sake hath forgiven you.

4. Memorize each part separately until you have memorized the entire verse.

Breaking tasks down into smaller parts is called microprogress. Instead of rushing toward a big goal and stumbling along the way, break that big goal into small, attainable goals—this makes the memory task more approachable. If you dread anything that requires a lot of memorization, breaking the task into small parts helps to keep you motivated. One small step at a time gets you to that big goal faster—and there's another reason to be joyful!

SELF-WORTH VS. TRUE WORTH

How do you measure your self-worth? Do you feel loved? Appreciated? Competent? Self-worth is often measured by what we believe others think of us, how well we think we fit in with those around us, and also our successes and failures. Measuring worth in that way means trouble. It allows Satan to rush in and fill our minds and hearts with lies. "Nobody loves me." "I'm not good enough." "I'm a terrible person." "I'm ugly...worthless...." Satan loves to build on negativity. And with each lie you believe, you allow him to pull you further from God.

True worth is different. True worth is seeing yourself through God's eyes and becoming the person He wants you to be. God made you in His image. He loves you all the time just the way you are. There is nothing you can do to stop Him from loving you, forgiving you, and helping you. When you let go of what the world thinks of you and what you expect from it and focus only on who you are in God's eyes, then you will discover true worth. It comes from being humble and knowing that you are precious in God's sight.

No one deserves what God has to give, but He gives anyway through His grace. Think about how much God values you. He loves you so completely that you don't need to worry about loving yourself. There is joy and peace knowing that God thinks you are worthy of Him. He loves you so much that He put your needs above those of His own Son, allowing Jesus to die on the cross so you can have eternal life and His love in heaven.

Measuring your self-worth by how many friends you have or how much money and success you've attained is prideful. When you give yourself credit, you set yourself above God, forgetting that you would have nothing without Him. But when you put aside worldly thoughts and focus on God and His love for you, you gain humility. You give up worrying about your self-worth and instead live every day trying to please Him. You take good care of yourself because you are His beloved child, and it makes God happy to see you happy and thriving.

Do you view your worth through the lens of God's eyes? Or do you allow people to determine your value? Striving to be good enough for someone else or the best at something is stressful and discouraging. But when you focus on the fact that you are precious to God, the way you see yourself is transformed. You know that you are loved, accepted, cherished—you are never alone. God is with you, and He is leading you toward something good.

Believe that you are good enough for God and that He has a great plan for your life. Find joy in Him, knowing that you need to do nothing—nothing at all—to earn His acceptance and love.

*And be ye kind one to another, tenderhearted, forgiving one
another, even as God for Christ's sake hath forgiven you.*
Ephesians 4:32

The Blank Page

"My dear friends, remember what you were when God chose you. The people of this world didn't think that many of you were wise. Only a few of you were in places of power, and not many of you came from important families. But God chose the foolish things of this world to put the wise to shame. He chose the weak things of this world to put the powerful to shame. What the world thinks is worthless, useless, and nothing at all is what God has used to destroy what the world considers important. God did all this to keep anyone from bragging to him. You are God's children. He sent Christ Jesus to save us and to make us wise, acceptable, and holy. So if you want to brag, do what the Scriptures say and brag about the Lord" (1 Corinthians 1:26–31 CEV).

Paul wrote those words to his friends at the church in Corinth. He reminded them that while the world thought of them as nothing, God used them to do something great. True wisdom, acceptance, and holiness came not through anything they had done, but through their relationship with Him.

Today, list five good things about yourself. Then give thanks to the Lord. Brag about the Lord to yourself or others. Brag about the wonderful things He has done to save you from self-worth and give you true worth.

The Last Word

Paul led many people to Christ, but he never bragged about his accomplishments. He says in 2 Corinthians 12:5 the only things he would brag about were his weaknesses. Paul believed that his weak spots were there to remind him not to become too proud.

When Paul asked the Lord to take away his weakness, the Lord said, "My grace is enough for you. When you are weak, my power is made perfect in you" (2 Corinthians 12:9 NCV). How did Paul respond to those words? He was joyful! "I am happy when I have weaknesses, insults, hard times, sufferings, and all kinds of troubles for Christ. Because when I am weak, then I am truly strong" (v. 10 NCV).

All of us have weak spots, specific things about ourselves that we don't like. Maybe it's a crooked tooth, shyness, fears, or a poor self-image.

Satan wants you to look in the mirror and cry. But God wants you to look in the mirror and be joyful. Why? Because He is enough for you! Your weak spots remind you that God's grace is sufficient. You are who you are today, and God loves you just as you are. You are His work in progress. Every day He is making you even better, shaping you into the person He wants you to be.

And be ye kind to *yourself*, tenderhearted, forgiving *yourself*, even as God for Christ's sake hath forgiven you.

THE PARTNER GOD WANTS ME TO BE

What every married person hopes for is a good, long, and stress-free relationship with his or her spouse. But in reality, most marriages go through rough spots. During those times, today's memory verse is one you can turn to: "And be ye kind one to another, tenderhearted, forgiving one another, even as God for Christ's sake hath forgiven you" (Ephesians 4:32). No one is perfect. Not you. Not your partner. Being kind, tenderhearted, and forgiving can be like a balm for a sore spot in your marriage.

What does God expect from you as a partner? Proverbs 31:10–31 provides an outline. It says a good wife is a precious treasure to her husband. He depends on her, and she is dependable. She keeps the household running smoothly and provides for her family's needs. Her skills are useful outside of the home. She is smart and capable. "She knows how to buy land and how to plant a vineyard. . . . She knows when to buy or sell" (vv. 16, 18 CEV). In today's world, she might be working in real estate or investments...or anything else! A Proverbs 31 woman is strong, graceful, cheerful, and positive. She gives sensible and thoughtful advice. She is never lazy.

She sounds like Superwoman, doesn't she? But working toward being a Proverbs 31 woman honors the Lord. The chapter ends saying that a woman who honors God deserves to be praised. She should be shown respect and praised in public for what she has done.

When your marriage hits a rough spot, remember to be the woman God wants you to be. Focus on the good things, and pray about what is not so good. Pray together with your spouse. Read the Bible, and listen to the words God speaks to you when you are quiet and conversing with Him in prayer. Think about what you expect from yourself in your marriage and what you expect from your partner. Ask yourself, "Does it fit with what the Bible says?" There are many scripture verses that speak to relationships (see 1 Peter 4:8; 1 Corinthians 13:7).

A strong Christian marriage is one in which both partners first focus on God and then on each other. It relies on God's mercy and grace. Commitment matters and vows are sacred. It encourages and concentrates on strengths instead of weaknesses.

When your marriage hits a sore spot, see if you can bring some joy into it. Sometimes all that's needed to move forward is a break from working on the problem and making time to do something you both enjoy.

Keep praying through those not-so-good times, and remember this—there is always hope in the Lord! "May the God of hope fill you with all joy and peace as you trust in him, so that you may overflow with hope by the power of the Holy Spirit" (Romans 15:13 NIV).

And be ye kind one to another, tenderhearted, forgiving one another, even as God for Christ's sake hath forgiven you.
Ephesians 4:32

The Blank Page

Try this little exercise. (You might get your partner to do it too.) Write the letters of your last name vertically on a piece of paper. Then for each letter write something that you and your spouse share. For example:

> M . . . marriage
> I . . . intimacy
> L . . . love
> L . . . life
> E . . . evangelism
> R . . . rest

If that was too easy, you might challenge yourself by using all the letters in the alphabet or both your first and last names.

When you have completed the exercise, you will have made a list of points where you and your partner connect. Concentrate on keeping those connections strong. Build on them and see if you can add even more words to your list.

The Last Word

What brings joy to a marriage? Obviously, spending time alone together is at the top of the list. Making time to be together, just the two of you, is key to communicating and keeping your connection strong. Being affectionate with each other is important too. Little things—a quick hug or kiss, some gentle words, even a smile—are affirmations of your constant love. Show gratefulness to each other. Remember to thank your partner often and especially for the little things. An unanticipated surprise can bring joy to a marriage, and so can celebrations. You don't need a reason to surprise your spouse or to celebrate. Just do it! Be playful. Find something new that you both enjoy, and pursue it together. Be spontaneous. Dance! Praise your partner, not only when you are alone together but also in public. Read scripture together and pray together. Psalm 126:3 (NIV) says, "The LORD has done great things for us, and we are filled with joy." End your days praising God for His goodness and also for each other.

Sometimes God gifts us with something unexpected that brings joy into our relationships. Other times, He wants us to be creative and find ways to bring joy to one another. Think about it: Where have you found joy in your marriage? What can you do to create some joy?

WALKING IN TRUTH

There is that special moment when a mother holds her child for the first time. Nothing compares with the joyfulness of a woman looking at her baby and imagining the future and all of the amazing firsts to look forward to.

Mary Ball Washington, George Washington's mother, was much like mothers today. She loved her son, George, and wanted the best for him. Mary's husband, Augustine, was often away on business, so the task of caring for George and his siblings fell totally on Mary. While Augustine was gone, Mary also had responsibility for overseeing the family's plantation.

She was a strong, independent woman, firm in her Christian faith. Mary taught her children Bible stories, and she used the Bible to teach them how to read and write. Christian behavior was paramount in the Washington household, and Mary lived her faith teaching by example. Even when Augustine died unexpectedly, leaving Mary as a single mom with five young children to raise, her faith remained strong.

When George, her oldest child, wanted his independence, Mary felt reluctant to let him go. Like most moms, the idea of the first child leaving home was almost too much for her. When young George wanted to join the navy, Mary said no. Too dangerous! George rebelled, which caused strain in their relationship.

Finally, when he was old enough to decide for himself, George joined the military and fought in the French and Indian War. His mother sent him off with these words: "Remember that God only is our sure trust. To Him, I commend you."

The rest, as they say, is history!

While George was fighting in wars and commanding armies, Mary was home worrying about him. Every day she went to her favorite quiet spot, a rocky place with shade trees and climbing vines, and she prayed for her son. At the same time, George was in prayer for his country. He had learned well from his mother to trust in God and walk in faith.

Third John 1:4 (NIV) is a scripture verse that Mary Washington might have read and memorized. It says, "I have no greater joy than to hear that my children are walking in the truth." This is the goal of all Christian mothers—to feel joy knowing that their children are walking in faith with the Lord.

Babies grow up, and the relationship between mother and child sometimes becomes strained. Just like George, children want their independence. Sometimes they rebel. But if you raise your children to love the Lord and set for them a good Christian example, like Mary Washington did, you can be sure that God hears the prayers you say for them.

Hold on to these words from 1 Samuel 1:27 (NLV): "I prayed for this boy [or girl], and the Lord has given me what I asked of Him." Stay strong in your faith. Ask God to lead your children to walk in the truth.

And be ye kind one to another, tenderhearted, forgiving one another, even as God for Christ's sake hath forgiven you.
EPHESIANS 4:32

The Blank Page

A prayer notebook is a great way to pray your children through life. Keep a small notebook with you, or you can use your smartphone as a recording device. Throughout each day, look for cues from your children about what they need. Is there a test at school that day or an important game after school? Make a note of it so you will remember to pray your child through it. Pray your children through the day. Pray for them when they get up in the morning, for safety on the way to school, for a good day of learning...pray them through all the way to bedtime! Also note things to pray for their future—to know the Lord and trust in Him, to resist temptation, to be an example of Christ to others...

Tell your children about your prayers for them. Explain why you pray for specific things. Teach them to pray for others. And every day be a good example of living a godly life.

When you and your child go through rough spots in your relationship, do what Mary Washington did—commend your child to God. Keep praying and trust God to do the rest.

The Last Word

Stock up on 3 x 5 notecards! They're inexpensive and great for memorizing longer scripture verses. Write each word of the verse on a separate card. Then put the cards in order. This helps train your brain not only to put the words in the correct order but also to visualize the verse.

Are you using the scripture verse index cards that come with this book? Remember to make them a part of your daily routine. Put the card on your bathroom mirror and practice the scripture while you do your hair and makeup. Take it with you and put it where you can see it throughout the day. Put memorizing it at the top of your to-do list. At bedtime, recite the scripture to God in prayer, and ask Him to help you apply it to your life. Allow scripture to be your guiding light.

Thy word is a lamp unto my feet,
and a light unto my path.
PSALM 119:105

Think about the joyful times you've shared with friends. One of the best things about friend relationships is that we choose our friends. As in all things, if we choose wisely, a good friendship lasts a lifetime. But true friendship stretches beyond joy. It is there in all circumstances. Proverbs 17:17 (NIV) says, "A friend loves at all times, and a brother [or sister] is born for a time of adversity." When a friend isn't joyful, when someone or something steals her joy, a good friend steps in. That friend knows there is a right time and way to help. The award-winning American author Octavia E. Butler put it this way: "Sometimes being a friend means mastering the art of timing. There is a time for silence. A time to let go and allow people to hurl themselves into their own destiny. And a time to prepare to pick up the pieces when it's all over."[5]

How are you at timing? Do you know when it's best to be silent? James wrote: "My dear brothers and sisters, always be willing to listen and slow to speak" (James 1:19 NCV). Sometimes, listening without giving advice is the best way to help a friend.

Listening requires patience and restraint. Listen to God when He leads you to be quiet. Good listening takes practice,

---

[5] Shane Croucher, "Who Was Octavia E. Butler? Quotes and Facts about Science Fiction Writer Celebrated in Google Doodle," *Newsweek*, June 22, 2018, https://www.newsweek.com/who-was-octavia-e-butler-quotes-and-facts-about-science-fiction-writer-990239.

especially when you see someone "hurling themselves into their own destiny." Even when your advice might be just what your friend needs, she might not be willing to listen, let alone heed what you have to say. Good listening requires concentration, truly hearing and trying to understand what your friend is saying. It means being attentive without distractions, listening with both ears and not interjecting your own experiences into your friend's story. In Philippians 2, Paul writes, "In your relationships with one another, have the same mindset as Christ Jesus" (v. 5 NIV). "Do nothing out of selfish ambition or vain conceit. Rather, in humility value others above yourselves, not looking to your own interests but each of you to the interests of the others" (vv. 3–4 NIV). Think about what your friend needs. If it is only a listening ear, then listen.

Like Octavia E. Butler said, being a friend means mastering the art of timing. If your friend asks for and is open to advice, offer it, but pray about it first. Ask God to give you the best words to say. If your friend won't listen, then continue praying, asking God to guide your timing. Be ready to pick up the pieces too, if it comes to that.

You are a good friend now, and you can be even better. You can be the kind of friend who brings joy to others by listening, understanding what's needed, and acting at just the right time.

And be ye kind one to another, tenderhearted, forgiving one another, even as God for Christ's sake hath forgiven you.
Ephesians 4:32

The Blank Page

Practice listening today. Talk less, listen more, and be understanding. Try to spend the whole day listening without interrupting. When you do speak, make it about the other person. Ask questions for clarity. Give affirmations that you are genuinely hearing what the other person is saying. Respond with positivity in both words and your facial expressions. Look at your friend while she speaks. If she pauses, concerned that she is talking too much, you can encourage her by simply saying, "I'm interested. Go on." If you struggle to focus on your friend's words, try repeating them in your head. Not only will this help you focus, but also it will reinforce to you what your friend is trying to say.

The next step takes even more practice, but give it a try: While your friend is speaking, listen for God's voice to you. Pray silently asking Him to lead you to hear and understand the message in your friend's words and to respond in the most helpful ways.

Good listening, like good timing, is an art, but it is one you can master with patience, practice, and a little help from the Lord.

The Last Word

The best example of friendship is your relationship with Jesus. Think of the endless hours He has listened to you as you poured your heart out to Him in prayer. Jesus already knows what you need. Still, He listens without interrupting your prayers. He listens. He hears. He genuinely cares. At just the right time, He will give you advice. It might come from reading the Bible, wise words spoken by a friend, or by Jesus Himself speaking to your heart. But always He waits until the timing is right.

Jesus is an example of the best kind of friendship, but He is much more than your friend. Jesus is Lord. His love for you never fails. He will never leave you or turn against you. Jesus says, "See! I stand at the door and knock. If anyone hears My voice and opens the door, I will come in to him" (Revelation 3:20 NLV). Always and especially when you need the help of a trusted friend, open the door to Jesus. He is waiting at the door, ready to come in. He will listen to your trouble and provide the help you need.

Week 3: DAY SIX

A WORLD OF GOOD

If you visit Rockefeller Center in New York City, you can see a famous art deco statue of the Greek god Atlas, holding the world on his shoulders. In Atlas's story, he led the Titans in war against the Olympic gods. The Titans lost, and Atlas was condemned to carry on his shoulders the weight of the earth and sky—a huge burden, indeed. Maybe at times you've felt like Atlas. Most people have.

You can't change the world and all the messiness Satan adds to it, but by changing how you relate to others you can get some of its weight off your shoulders.

Good or bad, a relationship is a connection. Sometimes you have a choice whether to connect with another person; sometimes you don't. But *how* you connect is always up to you. At work a difficult boss can make your life miserable. If you stay focused on God and scripture, you can give Him the weight of your cares. Ephesians 6:7–8 (NCV) is your go-to scripture for work: "Do your work with enthusiasm. Work as if you were serving the Lord, not as if you were serving only men and women. Remember that the Lord will give a reward to everyone, slave or free, for doing good." When work weighs heavy on your shoulders, remember that you are working for the Lord, and He will reward you for doing your best, even if your boss won't.

A positive, God-centered attitude is key to every relationship. Focusing on God and scripture changes how you relate to others. When burdensome, negative thoughts fill your head, get rid of them by applying Philippians 4:8 (NCV): "Think about the things that are good and worthy of praise. Think about the things that are true and honorable and right and pure and beautiful and respected." When a conversation turns sour, instead of allowing it to deteriorate, apply Proverbs 16:24 (NCV): "Pleasant words are like a honeycomb, making people happy and healthy." The Bible has an abundance of relationship advice, perfect for every situation.

How you relate to the world can do a world of good, not just for you but for others. How you interact with strangers, coworkers, friends, and family makes a difference. Your positive, God-centered attitude can be a powerful example of what it mean to be a Christian and live to please the Lord. Think of your attitude as a kind of ministry as you guide others by your example. Be kind to everyone, tenderhearted, and forgiving.

Hold on to the image of Atlas carrying the world on his shoulders, and when you feel as if the weight has shifted onto you, turn things around. The Bible says that anxiety weighs down the heart but a cheerful heart is good medicine. A cheerful heart is a joyful heart—a heart that brings joy to the world.

And be ye kind one to another, tenderhearted, forgiving one another, even as God for Christ's sake hath forgiven you.
EPHESIANS 4:32

The Blank Page

Check your attitude today. How do you react to negativity? When the world weighs you down, what do you do?

If you react with pessimism, you perpetuate it. You add more weight to the world. Norman Vincent Peale, who wrote *The Power of Positive Thinking*, said, "Repetition of the same thought or physical action develops into a habit which, repeated frequently enough, becomes an automatic reflex." You want your reactions always to be positive so they add joy to the world. Peale said, "Drop the idea that you are Atlas carrying the world on your shoulders. The world would go on even without you. Don't take yourself so seriously."

But how? How do you stop taking yourself and the world so seriously? One way is to remember that God is in charge. When you give your troubles to Him and sincerely trust that He has everything under control, you will shed some of the weight. When you stop measuring yourself against others and trust God with your future, that sheds weight too. Learn from your past mistakes and move forward. Add more humor to your life. Smile. Look for the things God puts in your path that make you laugh.

Practice being positive today. See if you can go through the entire day reacting only in positive ways and pushing negative thoughts from your mind.

The Last Word

If you are looking for an example of someone who found joy in the worst of circumstances, think first of Jesus. He suffered shaming, beatings, and crucifixion so in the end He would have the joy of fulfilling God's promise for us—so we could be with Him forever in heaven. Paul wrote in Hebrews 12:2 (NCV), "Let us look only to Jesus, the One who began our faith and who makes it perfect. He suffered death on the cross. But he accepted the shame as if it were nothing because of the joy that God put before him."

Paul, author of much of the New Testament, certainly had reason to complain—he was imprisoned, beaten, bullied, and berated—but still he kept a positive attitude. He knew how to find the good in things: "We are hard pressed on every side, but not crushed; perplexed, but not in despair; persecuted, but not abandoned; struck down, but not destroyed" (2 Corinthians 4:8–9 NIV). Paul added this advice: "Always be joyful and never stop praying. Whatever happens, keep thanking God because of Jesus Christ. This is what God wants you to do" (1 Thessalonians 5:16–18 CEV).

Jesus' brother, James, was another positive thinker. He said, "Consider it pure joy, my brothers and sisters, whenever you face trials of many kinds, because you know that the testing of your faith produces perseverance. Let perseverance finish its work so that you may be mature and complete, not lacking anything" (James 1:2–4 NIV).

Surround yourself with positive thinkers like Paul and James. Become one yourself. Let others see what it means to find joy in all circumstances just by trusting the Lord.

PUTTING IT ALL TOGETHER

Did you notice this week two common themes connecting the devotionals? Good relationships come from trusting the Lord and by maintaining a positive attitude even in negative circumstances.

Your relationship with God should be your first priority and then your relationship with yourself. If you aren't right with God and if you have unresolved issues with yourself, your other relationships will suffer.

Again, you can look to Paul as an example. He resolved his issues with God and himself. He went on to find joy in hardship and teach others to do the same.

When Paul was a young man, he was known as Saul. He saw Christians as his enemies and Jesus as a fraud. Saul found joy in the stoning of Jesus' follower Stephen and in the deaths of other Christians. But even then, God had a plan for Saul. Jesus appeared and confronted Saul as he traveled the road to Damascus. When Saul saw Jesus and heard Him speak, he trembled with fear knowing that he had been wrong. This was no fraud! Jesus was the promised Messiah. Saul believed, and he made the choice to follow Jesus. He repented and was baptized. Then he began the work of changing his thoughts and actions until in his old age he became one of the greatest Christians and teachers in the Bible. He was right with God and with himself.

Changing yourself for the better takes time. Although Paul's conversion to Christianity happened quickly, he remained God's work in progress. He gained wisdom as he followed the Lord's teachings and acted on them. In the worst of times, Paul remained the best of positive thinkers. He lived life to please God with the attitude that if he died for what he believed, he would receive the greatest reward—seeing God face-to-face and being with Him in heaven.

Read about Paul's conversion and early life as a Christian in Acts 9:1–30. Then read the other books Paul wrote, and discover the man Paul became by fixing his relationship with God and himself.

1 and 2 Thessalonians
Galatians
1 and 2 Corinthians
Romans
Ephesians
Philippians
Colossians
Philemon
1 and 2 Timothy
Titus

Paul was the most prolific of Bible authors, perhaps because of the time he spent in prison and the letters he wrote from there. By studying his words, you can learn much about forming a good relationship with God, yourself, and others. If you think of Paul as your mentor and heed his wise advice, you will not only find joy welling up in your heart, but you will discover an improvement in your relationships with others and with the world.

And be ye kind one to another, tenderhearted, forgiving one another, even as God for Christ's sake hath forgiven you.
Ephesians 4:32

The Blank Page

Satan doesn't want you to write scripture on your heart because then you can use it as a weapon when he tries to take away your joy. Every verse you memorize gives Satan less power in your life.

Satan lies. He wants to change your positive thoughts to negative. He is a sneaky character who masquerades as something good. He wants to lead you into sin. If you don't have God's words set firm in your heart, Satan can steal them from you. Read Mark 4:1–9, 13–20 and discover how Jesus explained the importance of memorizing God's Word. Knowing and acting on scripture brings only goodness, peace, contentment, and joy.

Relationship scriptures, such as this week's memory verse, Ephesians 4:32, when acted upon, heal relationships through kindness, tenderness, understanding, and forgiveness.

Be ready for Satan to try to harm your relationship with God, yourself, and others, but don't be afraid of him. Nehemiah 4:14 (NIV) is a good verse to remember when Satan tries to get in your way. "Remember the Lord, who is great and awesome, and fight for your families, your sons and your daughters, your wives and your homes."

Write God's Word on your heart. Fight for good relationships. Work toward making all of your relationships God-centered, joyful, and positive.

The Last Word

Heavenly Father, I want to strengthen my relationship with You, and I want You as a partner in every other relationship I have. Help me, please, to be right not only with You but also with myself. Change whatever needs to change within me so I will be a better reflection of Christ. Teach me to become a good listener and a positive thinker. Open my eyes to joy. Remind me, Father, that the weight of the world is on Your shoulders and not mine. In all my relationships, whether family, friends, coworkers, or strangers, lead me to be kind, tenderhearted, and forgiving. Amen.

Week 4
FINDING JOY
IN YOUR WORK

And whatsoever ye do, do it heartily,
as to the Lord, and not unto men.
Colossians 3:23

PREPARE YE THE WAY

When you hear the word *work,* what is the first thing that enters your mind? Did you say, "Joy!" If so, you are one of the few. Work is more often connected with negative thoughts and procrastination. "I have to work," is uttered apologetically. "I can't do (whatever fun thing you suggested) because I *have* to work."

This week we explore alternative ways of looking at work so you can turn "I *have* to work" into "I want to."

Colossians 3:23 is the starting point for discovering joy in your work. When you face a tough job, or when your tasks feel dull and unrewarding, remember who it is you are working for—the Lord! It is He who stands beside you at work, and He will reward you for a job well done. Colossians 3:24 (NIV) contains a promise: "You know that you will receive an inheritance from the Lord as a reward. It is the Lord Christ you are serving." That inheritance is heaven and being in Christ's presence forever. He gave His life for yours. So when you work as if working for Him, it is a form of praise. You are willing to tackle the hardest jobs with joy because Christ suffered far more to guarantee your forever joy in heaven. When you write Colossians 3:23 on your heart and then recall it at work, it will help you let go of negative thoughts about what you *have* to do and focus instead on Christ.

John the Baptist said, "Prepare the way for the Lord" (Matthew 3:3 NIV). When you get up in the morning, remember John's words. Prepare for your day as if preparing for Jesus.

Get into the habit of starting every morning with Him. Find a quiet place to pray, and ask Jesus to guide you through the day. Ask Him to be present with you at work and help you to have a right attitude and the ability to get the job done. After praying, make time to read scripture and a short devotional. Allow at least a half hour of uninterrupted time for prayer and devotion. The American evangelist R. A. Torrey wrote: "We are too busy to pray, and so we are too busy to have power. We have a great deal of activity, but we accomplish little. . .much machinery but few results."[6] Don't skip your morning time with Jesus. He is the One who leads you throughout the day.

Find joy in your preparation. In everything you do, praise God. When you get dressed, praise Him because you have clothes. When you make breakfast, praise Him for the food you eat. Give God thanks for your children as you get them ready for school. Thank Him for transportation to work. Praise God all the way to your workplace. If you do these things, then you'll be well prepared to tackle your work with joy.

And whatsoever ye do, do it heartily,
as to the Lord, and not unto men.
COLOSSIANS 3:23

---

[6] R. A. Torrey, *How to Obtain Fullness of Power in Christian Life and Service* (New York: Fleming H. Revell Company, 1807), 81.

The Blank Page

With Jesus at your side, you can approach each new workday with a clean slate. You've confessed your sins to Him, and He has already forgiven the mistakes you made yesterday and the times you procrastinated or approached tasks in a less-than-joyful way. Mentally erase yesterday's slate and start fresh. Here are some tips:

1. Arrive at work on time, or even a few minutes early.
2. Jot down your to-do list.
3. Prioritize your tasks.
4. Tidy up your work space.
5. Greet your coworkers cheerfully—joy is contagious!
6. Start sharp. Look and act like you are awake, present, and ready for the day.
7. Check your email, texts, and voice mail. Flag messages that need your immediate attention.
8. Imagine Jesus there at your side.
9. Say a quick prayer.
10. Get busy!

Continue to remember that Jesus is right there with you throughout the day. When you face a challenge, ask for His guidance. If work becomes dull, ask Him to help you stay focused. Jesus is the perfect boss, working alongside you, understanding your weaknesses and strengths, encouraging you and always helpful. Whatever you do, do it as if you are working for Him.

The Last Word

This week's memory verse should be easy to recall if you remember that Jesus is your work partner. Whatever kind of work you do, say the verse and imagine Him with you. If you work at a desk, Jesus is in the chair next to you. If you are a mail carrier, He walks with you every step of the way. If you drive to earn a living, Jesus is with you in the passenger seat. Imagine Him there. Talk with Him, and listen to Him speak to your heart. If you get called to a meeting, Jesus will go with you. He will guide your actions and your words. Your workday will be better—joyful even!—if you remember "Whatsoever ye do, do it heartily, as to the Lord, and not unto men."

Use a scripture card in this book. Put it where you can see it—on your desk, your dashboard, or your work space. Use it not only as a memory tool but also as a reminder that Jesus is with you all the time.

You might want to share the memory verse with your friends at work and tell them what you've learned from *Writing Joy on My Heart*.

Week 4: DAY ONE

SHOW ME THE WAY, LORD.

God has a calling for you. Do you wonder how you can serve Him through your work, how you can use the skills and talents He has given you? God might not give you a clear answer right away, but you can be sure He will guide you. He may steer you away from your present job and send you in a different direction, or He may plan for you to stay right where you are.

Kirk Cameron is an example of someone who was in the right occupation but not yet heeding God's call. Kirk grew up playing the character Mike Seaver on the hit television show *Growing Pains*. At a young age he had already attained material things that most people wouldn't have in a lifetime. A confirmed atheist, Cameron was far from living for and serving the Lord. But then he went to church with a girl he wanted to date. There he heard the Gospel for the first time. *What if there really is a God?* he wondered. Kirk invited Jesus to come into his heart. It changed him. He began living for Christ, and he never looked back. God already had Cameron in the profession He had chosen for him. Today, he produces and acts in Christian films. He also hosts a Christian television show, *The Way of the Master*. In everything he does, Kirk Cameron serves the Lord. He is always ready and willing to share Bible truths with others.

Joy happens when you find peace and purpose in your work. If you feel less than peaceful, then think about why. Examine your present work and identify how God is using you to meet specific needs. You might not be in a Christian profession working for the Church, but do the products or services your business provides enrich the lives of others? Then you might be exactly where God wants you. He might have you in a place where you are setting a Christlike example for others. Or He may be nudging you to move on, to work in a more godly profession, to start a business of your own, or train to learn something new.

Pray. Listen to the Lord. Ask Him to reveal His calling for your life. If you feel strongly that He is leading you away from where you are right now, don't be afraid to follow Him. Seek the advice of wise Christians. Ask them to pray with you and for you.

Until God leads you in a different direction, keep doing your job—do it as if you are serving the Lord. Ask God to grant you peace and also to help you accept that He has you exactly where He wants you at this moment in time. Ask Him to open your eyes to new ways to serve Him through your work. Then wait, and let God do the rest.

And whatsoever ye do, do it heartily,
as to the Lord, and not unto men.
COLOSSIANS 3:23

The Blank Page

Your calling might not come right away. God may put an idea in your head and grow it slowly until, eventually, you know you have to act on it. He may ask you to let go of something that gets in the way of you moving forward. In your present job, He might be preparing you for the next step by honing the skills you'll need.

Today, surrender your present life to God. Give Him control. Billy Graham said, "If you want a change in your life, if you want forgiveness and peace and joy that you've never known before, God demands total surrender. He becomes the Lord and the ruler of your life."[7] Surrender yourself to God unconditionally. Then trust Him to lead you to where He wants you to be.

Surrender is a daily choice. It is human nature to want to hold on. We want total control of our lives. But there are things we can't fix or change. Life happens. Surrendering to God means having complete faith in Him. It means trusting His promise in Jeremiah 29:11 (NIV): " 'For I know the plans I have for you,' declares the LORD, 'plans to prosper you and not to harm you, plans to give you hope and a future.' "

Spend time today in prayer surrendering to God. Ask Him to provide you with peace in your surrender and joy like you've never known before.

---

[7] Billy Graham, "A Message from Billy Graham: Total Surrender," *Decision* (January 2016), https://billygraham.org/decision-magazine/january-2016/a-message-from-billy-graham-total-surrender/.

The Last Word

Jesus asked His twelve disciples to leave their jobs and follow Him. Instead of choosing men who were already serving God as teachers, rabbis, or prophets, Jesus chose fishermen Andrew and Peter, and James and John who were not only fishermen but business owners adept at leading others. Jesus persuaded Matthew to give up his tax collector job. Tax collectors were despised by the Jewish people, considered extortionists and traitors. And He chose Simon, a zealot, a political activist with his mind set on a revolution. Each of these men, and the rest of the twelve, had specific talents and skills that Jesus would help them polish and eventually use to serve Him.

After His resurrection, Jesus appeared to His disciples and called them into service. He said, "Go and make disciples of all nations, baptizing them in the name of the Father and of the Son and of the Holy Spirit, and teaching them to obey everything I have commanded you." Jesus didn't just disappear into heaven and leave the disciples to their work. He made it clear that He was still their leader and their partner. He promised, "Surely I am with you always, to the very end of the age" (Matthew 28:19–20 NIV).

Listen for Jesus to call you. Follow where He leads you, and remember—whatever your calling, He will be with you every step of the way.

A PLACE FOR EVERYTHING

God is all about being organized and having a plan. Consider the story of Noah. God gave Noah specific instructions about how to build the ark. His instructions were detailed and organized so Noah had no problem understanding and following them:

> "So make yourself an ark of cypress wood; make rooms in it and coat it with pitch inside and out. This is how you are to build it: The ark is to be three hundred cubits long, fifty cubits wide and thirty cubits high. Make a roof for it, leaving below the roof an opening one cubit high all around. Put a door in the side of the ark and make lower, middle and upper decks.... You are to bring into the ark two of all living creatures, male and female, to keep them alive with you. Two of every kind of bird, of every kind of animal and of every kind of creature that moves along the ground will come to you to be kept alive. You are to take every kind of food that is to be eaten and store it away as food for you and for them." Noah did everything just as God commanded him. (Genesis 6:14–16, 19–22 NIV)

In Noah's story, God sets the perfect example of organization and efficiency.

Your goal is to model yourself after Noah and work as if

working for the Lord. To do that you need to rid yourself of any clutter that gets in the way of serving Him. When you work in an orderly way, you can serve God joyfully and efficiently.

Organization requires effort, and Satan will do everything in his power to keep you from putting things in order. Satan thrives in chaos. He loves clutter. It brings him joy if he can cause you to feel overwhelmed. He is happy when you procrastinate. Satan views disorganization as a chasm between you and the Lord, an open door for him to come into your home and your life. Maybe that's why the Bible warns, "Be sure that everything is done properly and in order" (1 Corinthians 14:40 NLT).

When you get organized, you create space to prioritize what is important. An organized work space allows you to be more productive because you spend less time digging through clutter. Organization relieves you of worry and stress. Instead of looking at piles of chaos and thinking, *I really need to do something about that*, you can get right to work and ask God, "What do You want me to do for You today?"

Marie Kondo, author of the bestselling book *The Life-Changing Magic of Tidying Up*, said, "People cannot change their tidying habits without first changing their way of thinking." Is anything cluttering your life and keeping you from serving the Lord? If so, then maybe it's time to dump the clutter. Change the way you think, and begin putting things in order. Do it as if you are working for the Lord.

And whatsoever ye do, do it heartily,
as to the Lord, and not unto men.
COLOSSIANS 3:23

The Blank Page

Begin removing the clutter from your life today. Instead of setting a big goal for getting organized, set small, attainable goals. Baby steps help build patience, and they also give you time to think through the decluttering process.

Sort through your items with two words in mind, *service* and *joy*. Ask yourself, *Does this item help me serve the Lord, my family, or myself? Is it a tool I can use to make my life or someone else's better? Does it bring enrichment or joy into my life or the lives of others?* If you answer yes to any of those questions, then keep that item.

Next, organize what you keep by putting it in a specific and logical place, someplace near where you need it. Use labels so you'll know where things are.

If you begin to feel stressed, tired, or overwhelmed—stop! Remember that Satan wants you to be discouraged and give up. Pray and ask God to lead you back to a place of refreshment and motivation.

With each small step you take toward getting organized, you will be closer to the end goal of working joyfully and efficiently while serving the Lord, your family, and others.

The Last Word

Clutter isn't only about things; it can also be thoughts that muddle your thinking and lead you away from God. Satan enjoys piling on negative thoughts, fearful thoughts, unclean or unhappy thoughts. Arm yourself with scripture so you can counter and conquer any thought that Satan puts in your head. Here are five scripture passages you'll want to remember. Use them to get yourself back on the pathway to joy.

- "We fight with weapons that are different from those the world uses. Our weapons have power from God that can destroy the enemy's strong places. We destroy people's arguments and every proud thing that raises itself against the knowledge of God. We capture every thought and make it give up and obey Christ" (2 Corinthians 10:4–5 NCV).
- "Set your minds on things above, not on earthly things" (Colossians 3:2 NIV).
- "Do not be shaped by this world; instead be changed within by a new way of thinking. Then you will be able to decide what God wants for you; you will know what is good and pleasing to him and what is perfect" (Romans 12:2 NCV).
- "For God hath not given us the spirit of fear; but of power, and of love, and of a sound mind" (2 Timothy 1:7).
- "For as he thinks in his heart, so is he" (Proverbs 23:7 NLV).

EVERYTHING IN ITS PLACE

Another key to finding joy is putting your priorities in order. The Bible is clear that God always comes first. In second place is your spouse, then your children and extended family, and after that your calling, your work. Even if the order gets shifted around sometimes, it is essential that God always comes first before any other relationship and in everything you do.

In the Ten Commandments, God puts Himself first. He says, "Thou shalt have no other gods before me" (Exodus 20:3). The message is obvious. You should never allow anyone or anything to take God's place at the top of your list. And you should work toward loving the Lord your God with all your heart and with all your soul and with all your strength and with all your mind (see Luke 10:27). When you build a strong bond with God, study His words in the Bible, and then apply them to your life, everything else begins to fall into place.

Your spouse is your next priority. Nothing and no one except God should get in the way of your relationship with your partner. This means you might have to give up or reorder certain commitments and interests to keep your marriage strong. The word *partner* is significant. The two of you are joined in a partnership called "marriage." A business risks failure if its partners don't give it enough attention or if they don't get along. The same is true for marriage. To have long-term success, marriage partners need to stay connected, communicate, work through troubles and toward common goals.

Family is in third place. When your relationships with God and your spouse are solid and when you learn and apply God's Word to your daily living, then you can count on the following: you will raise your children in a loving and God-centered home (see Proverbs 22:6), and you will set an example for your extended family, and everyone else, by doing what is good (see Titus 2:7).

Fourth in the list of priorities is your work. Be assured that Satan will tempt you to move this up on your list and put it above your relationships with your family, spouse, and even the Lord. Giving in to his temptation will rob you of joy. How can you keep this from happening? By making sacrifices. Completing a day's work and prioritizing God and your family might mean getting up earlier, going to bed later, or reducing the time you spend watching television or engaging with social media.

Keeping these priorities in place takes practice and commitment. C. S. Lewis wrote, "When I have learned to love God better than my earthly dearest, I shall love my earthly dearest better than I do now. . . . When first things are put first, second things are not suppressed but increased."[8] Do your best to set your priorities straight. Pray about it and ask God to help you.

And whatsoever ye do, do it heartily,
as to the Lord, and not unto men.
COLOSSIANS 3:23

---

[8] C. S. Lewis, quoted in Armand M. Nicholi Jr., *The Question of God* (New York: Free Press, 2002), 106.

The Blank Page

Today's application is one you and your spouse can do together. Grab a notebook and pen, then go someplace quiet where there are no interruptions. On the first notebook page, write the word *God*, on the second page *Us*, on the third *Our Family*, and on the fourth *Work*.

Think about how the two of you working together can make God the first priority in your marriage. On page one, write down the ideas you agree on.

On page two, identify places where your marriage needs work. Decide if you are giving your partnership the priority it deserves. If not, write down what you agree is getting in the way.

On the third page, write the subcategories *Kids*, *Parents*, *Extended Family*. Are any family relationships taking priority over your relationship with each other or with God? If so, what can the two of you do to reprioritize those relationships?

Finally, talk about work. Where is it on your priority list? How can you spend less time working and more time building your relationships with God, each other, and your children?

Don't limit this activity to one time. Plan alone time with your spouse for the purpose of building your priority plan. Then work the plan together.

The Last Word

Have you identified the technique that works best for your scripture memorization? Here's another you can try—make it a family affair! Here are a few ideas:

- Agree that you and your spouse will text the memory verse to each other three times during the day and text it from memory.
- Write the verse down and pack it in your spouse's or child's lunch bag.
- Play a family game. One family member hides this week's scripture card. That person chooses another family member to find it, but before he or she begins looking, that person has to recite the verse from memory. Young children really enjoy this game!
- Make it a competition. If every family member can recite the verse from memory at dinnertime, provide a special after-dinner treat. "And whatsoever ye do, do it heartily, as to the Lord, and not unto men" (Colossians 3:23).
- Be creative. See if your family can make up some other games or challenges for memorizing this week's verse.

WORKING FOR THE LORD

Work is important to God. We know this because after He created Adam, God gave him the task of tending the garden of Eden (see Genesis 2:15). Throughout the Bible, you will find God in partnership with others to do His work. Noah, for example, and Moses. One of the reasons God created humans was to care for His earth and everything in it. Through our sins, we humans made a mess of things, but God forgives us. He continues to use us to do His work here on earth.

Working for God is an honor. The Creator of the universe wants you to work for Him! What a privilege to be asked by the Boss of the world to work in His organization. Think about it. What would you say if God came down from heaven right now and said, "I want you to work for Me"? The truth is every day you have the opportunity to work for the Lord. Your job is to approach work ethically in ways that always honor Him. When you do your best work, even in the midst of criticism or without reward, God is pleased. The result of your work is not as important as the way you work. Your work, the decisions you make, the way you treat your bosses and coworkers should always be aligned with God.

This week's memory verse sums it up: "And whatsoever ye

do, do it heartily, as to the Lord, and not unto men" (Colossians 3:23). Webster's dictionary defines *heartily* this way: "with all sincerity; wholeheartedly; with zest or gusto; wholly; thoroughly." Can you honestly say that you work heartily, as to the Lord, in every kind of work you do? You can never meet God's standards. You are human, after all! But Colossians 3:23 sets the goal for your work. It reminds you about who you work for and how to work.

Yours is a weighty responsibility, being God's ambassador to earth. Still, you need time away from work to rest. The Scottish author and minister George Macdonald said, "It is our best work that God wants, not the dregs of our exhaustion. I think He must prefer quality to quantity." Make time daily to relax in the quiet and talk with your Boss in prayer. Talk with Him about your work, and ask Him to lead you. Ask Him how you can work to serve others. What can you do to help bring peace and well-being to your workplace and also the world? God gave you talents and skills. Ask God to help you use them to their fullest.

You might not understand right now how you are helping the Lord in your current job. But remember—the result of your work is in His hands, not yours. Work joyfully and heartily as if working for Him, and He will ensure that everything you do works out for the best (see Romans 8:28).

*And whatsoever ye do, do it heartily,
as to the Lord, and not unto men.*
COLOSSIANS 3:23

The Blank Page

Word association is an activity in which you write one or two words and then continue writing other words as they come to mind.

Write the words *God* and *work* on a piece of paper. Then write words, thoughts, and ideas that you associate with that word pair. Keep adding to your list for five minutes. Don't worry about what you write or overthink it. Just keep writing. When you are finished, review what you've written. This exercise will help you identify your feelings about God and work. It opens your eyes to new ideas. By doing this exercise, you might discover that you are beginning to view work in a different way or that you need to strengthen your partnership with God.

Try the activity again, this time using the words *serve* and *God*. Include random words along with thoughts and ideas. Then read and think about what you've written. Does it include some new ideas for serving the Lord?

Here are three other word pairs to try: *work* and *ethics*, *God* and *coworkers*, *work* and *joy*.

The Last Word

In his famous poem "I Hear America Singing," Walt Whitman paints a picture of workers singing while they work. Psalm 100:2 says: "Serve the LORD with gladness: come before his presence with singing." Listen. Can you hear them joyfully going about their work? Can you feel their continuing joy when the day's work is done?

I hear America singing, the varied carols I hear,
Those of mechanics, each one singing his as it should be blithe and strong,
The carpenter singing his as he measures his plank or beam,
The mason singing his as he makes ready for work, or leaves off work,
The boatman singing what belongs to him in his boat,
The deckhand singing on the steamboat deck,
The shoemaker singing as he sits on his bench, the hatter singing as he stands,
The wood-cutter's song, the ploughboy's on his way in the morning, or at noon intermission or at sundown,
The delicious singing of the mother, or of the young wife at work, or of the girl sewing or washing,
Each singing what belongs to him or her and to none else,
The day what belongs to the day—at night the party of young fellows, robust, friendly,
Singing with open mouths their strong melodious songs.

 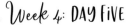

GOOD HOUSEKEEPiNG

Proverbs 31:10–31 outlines what it meant to be a "wife of noble character" in the Old Testament. Reading this "to-do" list would make most twenty-first-century wives want to run away from home. But still, there is wisdom in Proverbs 31. Verse 27 (NIV) says, "She watches over the affairs of her household and does not eat the bread of idleness." It is a verse you will want to remember.

There is an old English saying:

"Wash on Monday,
Iron on Tuesday,
Bake on Wednesday,
Brew on Thursday,
Churn on Friday,
Mend on Saturday,
Go to meeting on Sunday."

Puritan women brought this saying and their schedule of chores with them when they came to America on the *Mayflower*. For several hundred years, scheduled daily chores were expected from wives while their husbands went to work. If the chores weren't done completely and on time, well. . .that wife was "eating the bread of idleness."

But times have changed! The millennial wife is busier than ever. Household chores often give way to job responsibilities, transporting the kids here and there, volunteering, attending meetings at church, helping with homework. . . . She comes home to a pile of dirty laundry, a mess on the carpet, and a family asking, "What's for dinner?" Her spirits sink. She feels overwhelmed, maybe even angry.

Does that sound like you? There are ways to have a clean house and a joyful spirit. First, you have to watch over the affairs of your household and not allow idleness. In today's world, housework is teamwork. Set an example for your children of working for the Lord. Teach them this week's memory verse. Explain that they are to be helpers like Jesus' disciples. Assign them age-appropriate household chores and give them a say in which chores they most enjoy doing. Then find ways to make housework fun for the whole family—a challenge, a game, a hidden treasure—use the creativity God gave you. Finally, borrow some wisdom from the *Mayflower* women and set a routine. Do your best to follow it. Baby steps taken each day will result in a clean house on the weekend so you can relax and spend joyful time with your family without worrying about the mess at home. Remember also to provide praise and encouragement.

When you watch over the affairs of your household and do your best to promote a godly attitude about housework, you might receive the reward of Proverbs 31:28 (NIV): "Her children arise and call her blessed; her husband also, and he praises her." God doesn't expect you to be perfect, nor does He expect a perfectly spotless and orderly house. The most important thing is creating a clean, comfortable home, a home that draws family members closer to one another and to God.

And whatsoever ye do, do it heartily,
as to the Lord, and not unto men.
COLOSSIANS 3:23

The Blank Page

Here are some ways you can make chore time joyful for you and your family:

- Create a playlist of favorite songs to play while you and your family work together.
- Offer incentives. Make a weekly chart of goals and rewards. Try to avoid monetary rewards; instead choose rewards that promote togetherness, things you and your family can enjoy doing together.
- Make goals quick and easily attainable. Work toward a big goal by tackling it one day at a time.
- Hide prizes to be found while cleaning. Your kids will love this! It can be as simple as a note doubling as a coupon to go someplace fun, invite a friend for a sleepover, or choose one special treat on the next trip to the grocery store.
- Turn it into a game. Assign points for each household chore. When all the chores are complete, the person with the most points gets to choose a movie for the family to watch together or a board game to play.
- Purge unneeded items by holding a scavenger hunt. Have each family member find a set number of things that are taking up space and no longer needed. Put them together in a large tote. Then decide together which items to donate or put in the trash.

You might be amazed how rewarding housework can be if you present it as a family activity and do your best to make it fun.

Week 4: DAY SiX

The Last Word

If you think household chores are difficult today, consider what they were like in Bible times.

A woman rose before dawn and made a fire for cooking. She emptied chamber pots and drew water from a nearby stream or well. She mixed dough for bread and put it inside a clay or stone oven fueled by the fire she built. Then she ground flour for the next day's loaves. She swept the floors, mended, and also wove clothing for herself and her family. She cared for her children much the same as mothers do today. Her children drank milk, but usually not from cows. Their mother milked sheep or goats to provide their nutritious beverage. And if she had time, a mother might make her children a special treat of dried locusts drizzled with honey.

Chores were much more difficult then because women had only ancient tools. Women walked in all kinds of weather carrying water jars. Getting water today is easy. Just turn on the faucet! And instead of the conveniences of washers and dryers, clothes were washed in the stream and hung on branches to dry.

One thing hasn't changed. God still trusts women to watch over the affairs of the household. Today, praise Him for the chores you do, and thank Him for making them easier.

PUTTING IT ALL TOGETHER

What if God stopped working? The universe would come to a standstill and we wouldn't be here anymore. It is because of God's constant work and devotion to us that we exist. He doesn't sleep or take a vacation. Every work God does, He does for us because He loves us.

Show your appreciation by working as if you are working for Him. When we give ourselves totally to God and allow Him to guide us, God works through us to accomplish great things. In John 9:4 (NIV) Jesus tells His disciples, "As long as it is day, we must do the works of him who sent me. Night is coming, when no one can work." Until that day when the sun no longer shines and Jesus comes again, we must do the works of God.

This week, you have learned the importance of working for the Lord, being well prepared to work, identifying your calling, getting organized, and setting priorities. When you apply these principles to every work you do, and when you give the outcome to God, then without a doubt, you are working for the Lord.

Work is more than your job. It is how you approach daily living. In *everything*, work at it as if working for the Lord. You aren't working just for a paycheck or to move up in your profession. The most important reason you work is to bring glory to God.

Your work might not be easy; in fact, it could be very hard. But at the end of the day, if you believe you have served God and done His work, then you will have joy knowing you have pleased Him.

Whatever it is you do, whether you are a teacher, sell insurance, operate a machine, or drive a race car, you are a disciple of Christ working in that profession. You have a purpose, to bring God honor and glory. You accomplish that not only by doing your job well but also through your actions and words.

Part of working for the Lord is setting an example for others of what it means to be Christ's disciple. Being Jesus' disciple means giving up what you want and following Him. It means going where He wants you to go and doing what He wants you to do. It causes you to look at your work differently. You aren't just a teacher, an insurance agent, a machine operator, or a race car driver. You are God's representative in those professions. You are showing others what it means to be a disciple by serving them, treating them fairly, being helpful, loving, forgiving.

Colossians 3:24 promises a reward for those who serve the Lord. If you get nothing back from others for doing God's work, you can expect God's reward; "pressed down, shaken together, and running over, it will spill into your lap" (Luke 6:38 NCV).

And whatsoever ye do, do it heartily,
as to the Lord, and not unto men.
COLOSSIANS 3:23

The Blank Page

In 2 Timothy 3:16–17 (NIV), Paul writes, "All Scripture is God-breathed and is useful for teaching, rebuking, correcting and training in righteousness, so that the servant of God may be thoroughly equipped for every good work." Memorizing scripture is the most important tool you have when working for the Lord. It helps you prepare for work, get organized, and set your priorities. Memorizing scripture prepares you as a first responder to whatever you encounter in the workplace, whether it is to lead, to follow, to get along with your boss and coworkers, or to handle a crisis.

Scripture is authoritative, inspired by God, and always true. It is your Employee Handbook for work, trumping any other handbook. It equips you for serving the Lord in all that you do, and it helps you to work more efficiently.

You have learned about setting priorities and putting God first. Remember, putting Him first includes memorizing scripture. It is one key way that God communicates with you as He leads you in life and in your life's work.

One last tip for this week: Memorizing a scripture verse is not something you do just once. To keep from forgetting it, review the verse often by reading it in your Bible.

The Last Word

Father, teach me to be Your disciple. Show me how I can best serve You and others through everything I do. I want to work heartily and joyfully for You. Prepare me to work. Lead me to set my priorities straight and put You first in all things. Strengthen the skills You have given me, and help me to get organized so I can work efficiently for You. Lord, You have taught me that no job is too small or unimportant that I should not do it as if working for You. Reveal to me Your calling for my life. Whatever it is, wherever You want me to go, equip me with everything I need to serve You well. Amen.

Week 5

FINDING JOY IN DELIVERANCE

*Thou art my hiding place; thou
shalt preserve me from trouble;
thou shalt compass me about
with songs of deliverance.*

PSALM 32:7

DELIVER ME

In the Sermon on the Mount, Jesus taught His disciples how to pray.

Our Father which art in heaven, Hallowed be thy name.
Thy kingdom come, Thy will be done in earth,
  as it is in heaven.
Give us this day our daily bread.
And forgive us our debts, as we forgive our debtors.
And lead us not into temptation, but deliver us from
  evil: For thine is the kingdom, and the power, and the
  glory, for ever. Amen. (Matthew 6:9-13)

This is the prayer we remember, the model for all other prayers: to praise God first, then ask Him to meet our needs, ask for His forgiveness and to help us forgive others, to lead us away from Satan's temptations and to deliver us when Satan's evil intrudes on our lives. We pray the Lord's Prayer in church. We pray it also in times of trouble. We find comfort reciting Jesus' words, especially His final request to our Father: "Lead us not into temptation, but deliver us from evil."

Evil is all around us, but as Christians we trust God. We expect Him to keep evil away from us. Still, sometimes we end up facing it head-on. In those times, we can trust God to lead us through and deliver us to the other side where joy awaits. David says in Psalm 30, "At night we may cry, but when morning comes we will celebrate. . . . You have turned my sorrow into joyful dancing . . . . I will never stop singing your praises, my LORD and my God" (vv. 5, 11–12 CEV).

This week, we explore the topic of deliverance—God rescuing His people from danger. From beginning to end, the Bible is filled with stories of deliverance, stories that illustrate this week's memory verse, Psalm 32:7. There are stories about finding safety in God's presence when evil is all around—He is our hiding place. Stories about avoiding evil by the grace of God—He preserves us from trouble. And stories about God leading His people through evil—He compasses us about and delivers us to a safe place filled with joyful song.

God is ready to deliver us today just as He delivered His people long ago. Whether we face fire like Shadrach, Meshach, and Abednego; are thrown into a den of hungry lions like Daniel; or walk through the valley of the shadow of death, God is present with us. He says, "Call on me in the day of trouble; I will deliver you, and you will honor me" (Psalm 50:15 NIV).

Get in the habit of praying for and trusting in God's protection and His deliverance. He is faithful, always present, saving us through His grace. Whether it comes in this life or in heaven, God promises us a place where trouble ends with dancing, and sadness with a joyful song.

Thou art my hiding place; thou shalt preserve me from trouble; thou shalt compass me about with songs of deliverance.

PSALM 32:7

The Blank Page

When trouble comes, you can always pray using the Lord's Prayer as a model. Today, try personalizing the Lord's Prayer, making it your own.

"Dear heavenly Father, no one is more holy than You. No one is more worthy of praise and honor. I look forward to the day when Jesus comes back to establish His kingdom here on earth. Father, I ask for Your will to be done in my life. I am worried about (your own words here). I need (tell God what you want from Him). I am a sinner, Lord. Please forgive me and help me to forgive others. Lead me to stay focused on You so I will watch out for and avoid temptation. If evil does enter my life, then deliver me through Your mercy and grace to a place of peace and joy. Amen."

You don't have to say those exact words. Just remember to include all the elements of Jesus' model prayer:

- Acknowledge God as the One and Only.
- Praise Him.
- Acknowledge that Jesus is coming again to set up God's kingdom on earth.
- Ask that God's will, and not your own, be done in your life.
- Ask Him to provide for your needs.
- Ask for forgiveness for your sins and for God to help you forgive others.
- Ask Him to help you to avoid temptation and to deliver you from any evil that gets in your way.

The Last Word

You might have memorized scripture without knowing it. If you can say the Lord's Prayer from memory, then you have memorized Matthew 6:9–13 and Luke 11:2–4. Maybe you also memorized "The Lord is my shepherd" from Psalm 23, or the Ten Commandments (Exodus 20:3–17); and almost every Christian can recite John 3:16: "For God so loved the world, that he gave his only begotten Son, that whosoever believeth in him should not perish, but have everlasting life."

Do you recall the method you used to memorize these well-known scripture passages? It's likely they stayed with you because you heard them said many times as a child in Sunday school and as an adult in church.

When you memorize scripture, apply it and use it in everyday life. The more you use it, the greater your ability to recall.

This week's memory verse is a go-to verse for whenever Satan tries to block your way. Every time you feel afraid or worried, if negative events in the world get you down, recite Psalm 32:7: "Thou art my hiding place; thou shalt preserve me from trouble; thou shalt compass me about with songs of deliverance." Before long, it will become as familiar to you as the Lord's Prayer, the Twenty-Third Psalm, and the Ten Commandments.

WHEN YOU WALK THROUGH THE FIRE

If you read Daniel 3, you will discover one of the Bible's most miraculous deliverance stories. It happened when King Nebuchadnezzar ruled Babylon. The king ordered a huge gold statue to be built in a valley near the city. Its purpose? To give glory and honor to the king's false god. Nebuchadnezzar ordered his subjects to bow to the statue when they heard some special music play. If they disobeyed, there were terrible consequences. Those who did not bow to the statue were doomed to be thrown into a red-hot fiery furnace. Three Jews, all holding high positions in the Babylon province, disobeyed the king's orders. Shadrach, Meshach, and Abednego would only bow to the One true God. Nebuchadnezzar gave them a second chance to worship his god, but the men refused.

> *"If you don't, you will at once be thrown into a flaming furnace. No god can save you from me."*
>
> *The three men replied, "Your Majesty, we don't need to defend ourselves. The God we worship can save us from you and your flaming furnace. But even if he doesn't, we still won't worship your gods and the gold statue you have set up." (Daniel 3:15–18* CEV)

Their fate was sealed. Shadrach, Meshach, and Abednego

were tied up and thrown into the furnace. But they were not alone.

"Weren't only three men tied up and thrown into the fire?" the king said. "I see four men walking around in the fire. . . . None of them is tied up or harmed, and the fourth one looks like a god" (vv. 24–25 CEV). The king ordered the men to come out. They were not burned, their hair wasn't scorched, and their clothes didn't even smell like smoke. The One and only God was with them.

Shadrach, Meshach, and Abednego believed in God's promise of deliverance. Even if God chose for them to die in the fire and be with Him in heaven, the three men were okay with His choice.

We can compare this event in ancient Babylon to world events today. Wildfires sometimes break out in residential areas. The fire spreads fast. Homes and lives are threatened. But God sends firefighters to walk through the inferno, rescuing people, delivering them from the heat and flames. If tragically some do not get out, if they are not delivered by God here on earth, He will deliver those who believe in Him through the gates of heaven and into the joy of His presence.

God promises in Isaiah 43:2 (NKJV), "When you pass through the waters, I will be with you; and through the rivers, they shall not overflow you. When you walk through the fire, you shall not be burned, nor shall the flame scorch you." God wants you to have unwavering faith like Shadrach, Meshach, and Abednego so when you face trouble, you can genuinely say: "The God I worship can save me. But even if He doesn't. . ."

Thou art my hiding place; thou shalt preserve me from trouble;
thou shalt compass me about with songs of deliverance.
PSALM 32:7

The Blank Page

One of Satan's greatest joys is robbing us of faith, especially in troubled times. Faith is important to God. It is the foundation on which we build our relationship with Him, and Satan wants to destroy it.

To have true faith, you first have to believe that God exists. He is the cornerstone of the foundation. Next, believe that the Bible is His letter to you and everything in it is true. Work to build trust in His promises, and pray asking God to increase your faith.

In one of Charles Schulz's cartoons, Charlie Brown says to Snoopy, "Are you upset, little friend? Have you been lying awake worrying? Well, don't worry...I'm here....The flood waters will recede, the famine will end, the sun will shine tomorrow, and I will always be here to take care of you!"[9] Our pets rely on us. We reassure them through words and actions that we will care for them. If that trust exists between us and pets, then why is it so hard to have faith in God?

In Isaiah 46:4 (NIV), God says, "Even to your old age and gray hairs I am he, I am he who will sustain you. I have made you and I will carry you; I will sustain you and I will rescue you." Think about that today. Then do your best to live each day believing by faith that God is taking care of you.

---

[9] Charles Schulz, "Peanuts," comic strip, Fandom, July 1993, https://peanuts.fandom.com/wiki/July_1993_comic_strips.

The Last Word

Read Daniel chapter 3.

Did you notice that Shadrach, Meshach, and Abednego didn't give in when others around them did? King Nebuchadnezzar, a powerful leader, ruled by intimidation and fear. When he commanded his people to listen to his music and bow to his false god, they did. They denied the One true God and bowed instead to a golden statue because fear made them do it. Imagine the joy Satan, the god of fear, felt when the people of Babylonia marched into sin because they were afraid of their earthly king.

We live in a world where many still march to the beat of Nebuchadnezzar's music. It is so loud we can't ignore it. But we can choose not to sing along. As Christians, if we have faith in the One and only God, we walk through the fire believing that He will take care of us. We accept that the fire might destroy our bodies, and we hold on to the words of Jesus, who said, "Do not fear those who kill the body but cannot kill the soul. But rather fear Him who is able to destroy both soul and body in hell" (Matthew 10:28 NKJV).

YOU AND GOD AGAINST THE WORLD

We all have days when it seems the whole world is against us. The prophet Daniel certainly felt that way when he served under King Darius.

As a young boy Daniel, an Israelite, was brought as a slave to Babylon. He grew up there working for several kings—all of whom did not believe in God. Daniel never gave up his loyalty to the One true God, nor did he participate in anything that went against Him. In spite of his allegiance to God, the kings respected Daniel for his wisdom and relied on his ability to prophesize and interpret dreams. They gave him positions of power in their kingdoms.

Daniel was an old man by the time Darius was king. Darius liked Daniel and he allowed him to worship God as he pleased. But Daniel had enemies, men who despised his wisdom and good relationship with the king. They plotted to get rid of Daniel. The men went to Darius and proposed a plan that for thirty days no one could pray or make requests to anyone other than the king. Darius wanted his subjects to obey and worship him, so he signed the idea into law. If anyone disobeyed, their fate was a den of hungry lions.

Of course Daniel wouldn't obey such a law. He continued

praying to God. His enemies had him arrested, and although Darius liked Daniel—his law was the law. Daniel was thrown to the lions, but the king regretted his ruling. He didn't sleep that night. In the morning, Darius went to the lions' den wondering if, maybe, Daniel's God had saved him.

"[The king] shouted, 'Daniel, you were faithful and served your God. Was he able to save you from the lions?' Daniel answered, 'Your Majesty. . .my God knew that I was innocent, and he sent an angel to keep the lions from eating me'" (Daniel 6:20–22 CEV).

When it seems everyone is against you, God will be on your side as He was Daniel's. Shut out voices that urge you to sin. Worship and pray only to God and He will deliver you.

God is present with you in the worst of circumstances. Maybe you lost a job while coworkers thrived. Maybe someone you trusted turned against you. Maybe Satan hit you with multiple hardships all at once. Still, God was with you!

There is joy in God's presence. James wrote, "Consider it pure joy, my brothers and sisters, whenever you face trials of many kinds, because you know that the testing of your faith produces perseverance" (James 1:2–3 NIV). Daniel knew that kind of joy. Even when it seemed everyone was against him and when his faith was tested, Daniel persevered. He kept trusting his God and, ultimately, he experienced a joyful delivery from the lions' den.

God is present with you too—always. Trust in Him the way Daniel did. He won't let you down.

Thou art my hiding place; thou shalt preserve me from trouble; thou shalt compass me about with songs of deliverance.

PSALM 32:7

The Blank Page

Daniel trusted in God's presence in the worst of circumstances. His story is a testament to God's faithfulness. Daniel never conceded his standards. He stayed true to God. Even when everyone else worshipped false gods and bowed to the king, Daniel trusted God to deliver him from evil.

Today, think about your principles and values.

1. Are your principles and values aligned with what you know God expects from you?
2. Do you hold on to your Christian values and beliefs in all circumstances?
3. How easily are you influenced when others want you to join in with something you know God disapproves of?
4. On a scale of one to ten, how firm is your faith in God?
5. Would you risk death to stay true to Him?
6. How do you react in hard times?
7. Do you trust God to deliver you?
8. What can you do to build a Daniel-like relationship with God?

God is with you always. He knows your thoughts, actions, and the degree to which you trust Him.

The Last Word

Habakkuk 3:17–19 is a beautiful scripture passage about joy in hard times and trusting in God's deliverance. The Old Testament prophet wrote: "Although the fig tree shall not blossom, neither shall fruit be in the vines; the labour of the olive shall fail, and the fields shall yield no meat; the flock shall be cut off from the fold, and there shall be no herd in the stalls: yet I will rejoice in the LORD, I will joy in the God of my salvation. The LORD God is my strength, and he will make my feet like hinds' feet, and he will make me to walk upon mine high places."

Finding joy in hard times comes from believing that God is the source of your salvation. Jesus is your promise of forever, joyful life in God's presence. There is joy knowing that God gives you strength to endure hardships. He delivers you from your valleys. He lifts you up the way a swift deer is able to easily climb to high places.

Remember Habakkuk's words when trouble enters your life. God is with you, and He understands. He is faithful to make you strong and help you move forward toward joy.

GREAT IS HIS FAITHFULNESS

God can be trusted to provide what is right for you in all circumstances. He is faithful. He is present with you, watching over you and listening when you pray. No need is too small or too trivial to Him.

Exodus 16 tells about the Israelites' need for food as they traveled to the Promised Land. They were fifty days into their journey and starving. The people grumbled to Moses wishing they had never left Egypt where there were pots of meat and all the food they wanted. Their faith in God and in Moses fell apart. God saw how weak their faith was. Still He provided for their needs. He spoke to Moses. "I have heard the grumbling of the Israelites. Tell them, 'At twilight you will eat meat, and in the morning you will be filled with bread. Then you will know that I am the LORD your God'" (v. 12 NIV). That evening, a huge flock of quail landed in their camp. In the morning, bread rained down from heaven. It was a very big deal because it saved the whole tribe of Israelites from starving to death. They praised God joyfully for a while. But as the Israelites' story continues, we discover many times when their faith in God waned.

By comparison, Charles Spurgeon shared in a sermon this story about his grandfather James Spurgeon, a rural pastor who always trusted in God. James had a large family and a small income. One day the family's cow died. The Spurgeon children had relied on the cow for milk, and James's wife was worried. But James was not. "God said He would provide, and I believe He could send us fifty cows if He pleased," James said. God honored James's strong faith. That same day church leaders, whom James didn't know, met in London to allocate money to low-income pastors. They neared the end of their list with just five pounds remaining. One of the men suggested sending it to James Spurgeon, not knowing that James was in dire need of a cow. Another added an additional five pounds. Others joined in, and the day after the cow died James received twenty pounds in the mail! The need of one cow might have seemed small, but to the Spurgeons it meant everything. God provided what they needed and more! Because James had been faithful to God, God was faithful to him.

When God provides, we find joy in His faithfulness. "Great is the LORD and most worthy of praise" (Psalm 145:3 NIV). In one of the most well-known hymns ever written, Thomas Chisholm penned these words:

> *"Great is Thy faithfulness,*
> *Great is Thy faithfulness,*
> *Morning by morning new mercies I see;*
> *All I have needed Thy hand hath provided*
> *Great is Thy faithfulness, Lord unto me!"*

Praise God today. Praise Him every day for meeting your needs.

Thou art my hiding place; thou shalt preserve me from trouble;
thou shalt compass me about with songs of deliverance.

PSALM 32:7

The Blank Page

Today's challenge is to think about the past seven days and list the times when God met a specific need. Consider times when God met your need without intervention from others. For example, a time when you found something you thought you lost or an ingredient for cooking you thought you didn't have. Think also about times when He met your needs through others. Maybe you dreaded preparing a meal for your family after you'd spent a tiring day at work, and your spouse called spontaneously suggesting you all go out for dinner.

God supplies countless little miracles every day. Open your eyes to them. Whenever you discover one, immediately praise God. Noticing the small ways He meets your needs helps build your faith in Him, so when a big need comes along your trust in Him is strong.

Our heavenly Father already knows what you need before you ask. You can trust Him to provide exactly what you need when He knows you need it. You might not always understand His timing and the method by which He meets a need. But always you can trust God's faithfulness to provide what is best.

"For your Father knows the things you have need of before you ask Him" (Matthew 6:8 NKJV).

The Last Word

Sometimes memorizing scripture is easier if you study and meditate on its content. What is the general message of the verse? How have other Christians interpreted it and applied it to their lives?

A quick online search leads to a list of commentaries or sermons for most verses. A deep study of a Bible verse makes it likely that you will not only remember its words, but also apply its message to your own personal situations.

Try it with this week's verse: "Thou art my hiding place; thou shalt preserve me from trouble; thou shalt compass me about with songs of deliverance" (Psalm 32:7).

God is always faithful, but His timing isn't ours. We walk through valleys longer than we think we should. Our faith in God is tested, diminished, or lost altogether.

What does God want from us in the valleys? He wants us to soldier on—continue even when it's difficult.

While Paul was in prison, he wrote to his friend Timothy, "Share in the troubles we have like a good soldier of Christ Jesus. A soldier wants to please the enlisting officer, so no one serving in the army wastes time with everyday matters" (2 Timothy 2:3–4 NCV). Paul reminded Timothy that instead of worrying about his circumstances, he should keep his mind centered on God.

It's hard to keep your mind on God's faithfulness and to trust in His deliverance when your world is falling apart. But God says it is possible. He even provides us with an armor of protection. Paul describes it like this: "You need to put on God's full armor. Then on the day of evil you will be able to stand strong. And when you have finished the whole fight, you will still be standing. So stand strong, with the belt of truth tied around your waist and the protection of right living on your chest. On your feet wear the Good News of peace to help you stand strong. And also use the shield of faith with which you can stop all the burning arrows of the Evil One. Accept God's salvation as your helmet, and take the sword of the Spirit, which is the word of God. Pray in the Spirit at all times with all kinds of prayers, asking for everything you need. To do this you must always be ready and never give up" (Ephesians 6:13–18 NCV).

Paul said our fight is against spiritual wickedness—Satan's attempts to keep us from climbing out of the valleys. But if we put on God's full armor, we will be strong enough to fight and win.

This week's memory verse says God "shalt compass me about with songs of deliverance." God is your compass; He points the way out of the valley. It might be a tough journey, but God promises you joyful songs of deliverance. The prophet Isaiah said a time is coming when "every valley shall be raised up, every mountain and hill made low; the rough ground shall become level, the rugged places a plain" (Isaiah 40:4 NIV).

Maybe today you are in a valley. Don't lose faith. Soldier on! Put on the armor of God, and continue to pray asking God for what you need. Until He delivers you from the valley, wear His armor of protection. With all your strength fight the evil one. Remember you are a soldier in God's army. God is with you. He will never leave you alone in the valley.

Thou art my hiding place; thou shalt preserve me from trouble; thou shalt compass me about with songs of deliverance.
PSALM 32:7

The Blank Page

Start teaching your children today how to soldier on through their difficulties—getting a shot at the doctor's office, a challenging day at school, or getting along with others. Use the valleys as teachable moments. Prepare your children to trust in God to help them do something even when it's difficult.

When young children are able to understand, teach them about the parts of God's armor: truth, right living, peace, faith, salvation, the Word of God, and prayer. You don't have to teach the parts all at once. Introduce them one at a time as your child is ready. Explain what each part of God's armor does. Use examples of situations in their lives where a specific armor part might be needed.

Remind your children to put on their armor every day. Make it fun! Have them pretend to put the armor on while naming its parts. When your children learn how to soldier on, they will be well equipped as adults to get through life's valleys.

The Last Word

During World War II Corrie ten Boom and her family hid in their home Jewish people hunted by the Nazis. Eventually the Ten Booms were caught, arrested, and put into a prison camp. Life in the camp was almost unbearable, but still Corrie held tight to her faith in God. She ministered to others in the camp and taught them about Jesus. When Corrie was finally released, she wrote a book about her experiences. *The Hiding Place* continues to be a bestseller and Corrie a stellar example of faith.

Corrie ten Boom said, "There is no pit so deep that God's love is not deeper still." She understood that in trouble, God was her hiding place. He was the One she ran to for protection, comfort, and love. Make God your hiding place. Keep soldiering on, allowing Him to lead you. Put your fate in His hands. Here are a few more inspiring quotes from Corrie:

"Don't bother to give God instructions, just report for duty."

"The first step on the way to victory is to recognize the enemy."

"In darkness God's truth shines most clear."

THE DEEPEST VALLEY

Our hearts ache when we lose a loved one. There is no joy in the deepest of valleys. To find it again, to be delivered out of grief, we need to look forward and also back.

We can look back to when Jesus lived on earth and see that He understood grief. Jesus wept over the death of His friend Lazarus. He shared the pain of Lazarus's family and friends over the loss of their beloved. Jesus understood compassion—He healed the sick, the lame, and raised the dead. Does He still have power to heal? Yes. Sometimes miracles happen. We don't know why more people don't receive healing, but we can be somewhat satisfied and always comforted knowing that Jesus loves us. He wants us to feel His love and compassion especially in times of sorrow. When a death brings sadness, we can look back and be sure Jesus understands how we feel.

The Bible says God keeps a record of our sorrows. He collects our tears and puts them in a bottle (see Psalm 56:8). He sees when we cry. He understands our pain. In times of death we see that others came to help. Whether they helped with arrangements, brought food, or came ready with hugs and prayers, these people were God's hands in human bodies. Looking back, we see God meeting our needs through the actions of family members, friends, neighbors, and even strangers. We see that God has been faithful. We know we can trust in His faithfulness again to deliver us from sadness.

Looking forward, we see the ultimate place of healing—heaven—our forever home. We remember that our time on earth is temporary and look forward to the day when we can be together again with our loved ones. While we remain apart from them our grief diminishes. We know we will never stop missing those who are no longer with us, but because God loves us, grief will eventually find its place. The pain will heal leaving a scar, but we will move on with our lives. Joy will return. We will laugh again and be happy.

Healing from a loss takes time. God understands. We all process grief in our own ways. Ecclesiastes 3:1–4 says, "To every thing there is a season, and a time to every purpose under the heaven: a time to be born, and a time to die. . .a time to heal; a time to break down. . .a time to weep, and a time to laugh; a time to mourn, and a time to dance."

God understands grief and pain, and if we hold tightly to Him, we can trust that He will heal our sorrow and deliver us into a new place of joy.

Thou art my hiding place; thou shalt preserve me from trouble; thou shalt compass me about with songs of deliverance.
PSALM 32:7

The Blank Page

Meditating on the following scriptures can bring comfort in sad times. Write them on your heart.

- "Weeping may endure for a night, but joy cometh in the morning" (Psalm 30:5).
- "The LORD is close to the brokenhearted and saves those who are crushed in spirit" (Psalm 34:18 NIV).
- "Blessed are they that mourn: for they shall be comforted" (Matthew 5:4).
- "Very truly I tell you, you will weep and mourn while the world rejoices. You will grieve, but your grief will turn to joy" (John 16:20 NIV).
- "Now is your time of grief, but I will see you again and you will rejoice, and no one will take away your joy" (John 16:22 NIV).
- "He heals the brokenhearted and binds up their wounds" (Psalm 147:3 NKJV).
- "They that sow in tears shall reap in joy" (Psalm 126:5).
- "Jesus then said, 'I am the one who raises the dead to life! Everyone who has faith in me will live, even if they die'" (John 11:25 CEV).
- "O Lord my God, I will give thanks to You with all my heart. I will bring honor to Your name forever. For Your loving-kindness toward me is great. And You have saved my soul from the bottom of the grave" (Psalm 86:12–13 NLV).
- "You changed my sorrow into dancing. You took away my clothes of sadness, and clothed me in happiness" (Psalm 30:11 NCV).

The Last Word

The Reverend Luther F. Beecher, a nineteenth-century New England preacher, wrote the comforting poem "What Is Dying?" comparing death to a ship traveling over the horizon. It reminds us that believers continue to live after death. When loved ones die and leave our sight, they are delivered to a joyful reunion on the other side.

I am standing upon the seashore. A ship at my side spreads her white sails to the morning breeze and starts for the blue ocean. She is an object of beauty and strength, and I stand and watch her until she hangs like a speck of white cloud just where the sea and sky come down to meet and mingle with each other. Then someone at my side says: "There! She's gone!" Gone where? Gone from my sight—that is all. She is just as large in mast and bull and spar as she was when she left my side, and just as able to hear her load of living freight to the place of her destination. Her diminished size is in me, and not in her. And just at that moment when someone at my side says: "There! She's gone!" there are other eyes that are watching for her coming; and other voices ready to take up the glad shout: "There she comes!"

And that is—"dying."

PUTTING IT ALL TOGETHER

If God is ready to deliver us, if we can always count on Him, then why is it so hard to trust Him? Believers have struggled with this question since the beginning of time. When the serpent promised wisdom to Eve, she ate God's forbidden fruit instead of trusting in God's wisdom and instructions. When God promised a childless Sarah that she would give birth in her old age, Sarah laughed. She didn't trust in God to do the impossible. When Job's wife saw him clinging to his faith even after he'd lost everything, she told Job to give up. "Curse God and die!" she said. Job's wife didn't trust in God's deliverance. We struggle with the idea of trusting God because we too often compare Him only with what we know. When we step into the unknown, our faith crumbles.

That is when Satan finds us. He leads us into temptation and mistrust. We ask, "Why didn't God deliver me from this bad situation? Where was He when I needed Him?" The answer is God was with us all the time. Maybe we got in God's way while He was trying to help us and that resulted in a longer stay in the valley. Or God had a better plan with a different timeline than our own and our impatience led to shattered faith.

This week, you read powerful examples of faith: Shadrach, Meshach, and Abednego; Daniel; James Spurgeon; Corrie ten

Boom. . . . All faced life-threatening situations, and they trusted God enough to put their lives in His hands. They trusted God to deliver them out of their valleys, and even if they died, they understood death as a form of deliverance. They believed that nothing could harm them in God's presence. If their bodies died, their souls would continue to live present with the Lord. That is the kind of trust God wants us to have. He wants us to put on His armor and soldier on through battles. Like soldiers following the commands of their leaders, God wants us to follow His commands and trust in His leadership.

When our faith wears thin, we can run to God for rest and refreshment. He is our hiding place. In good times, we ask Him to preserve us from trouble and praise Him for His blessings. In bad times, we should trust in His deliverance and, like Job, not give up even when others tell us to.

The great preacher and chaplain of the US Senate Peter Marshall said, "God will not permit any troubles to come upon us, unless He has a specific plan by which great blessing can come out of the difficulty." If you are in a troubling situation today and are worried about the unknown outcome, remember—you don't serve an unknown God! He loves you. He wants to deliver you from everything evil. God is good and faithful. Trust Him.

Thou art my hiding place; thou shalt preserve me from trouble; thou shalt compass me about with songs of deliverance.

Psalm 32:7

The Blank Page

Memorizing scripture is important because it reminds us of who God is. He loves us. God is faithful. He is always with us, going before us, guiding and redirecting us. God is our hiding place when trouble overwhelms us or when we feel afraid. He is our comfort in sadness. God collects our tears and keeps a record of our sorrows. He leads us away from temptation, and He delivers us from evil. When we memorize scripture, especially verses about God's character, we open our hearts wider to receive even more of Him. We build trust in Him as our loving Father who wants for us what is best.

In this week's memory verse, King David praises God for releasing him from suffering. His soul rejoices in God's grace as he meditates on God's loving character. "Thou art my hiding place; thou shalt preserve me from trouble; thou shalt compass me about with songs of deliverance" (Psalm 32:7). As you memorize this verse, be like David. Meditate on who God is, and find joy in His grace, mercy, and love.

The Last Word

Dear God, I praise You! Thank You for never leaving my side. You are with me always, in good times, in times of trouble, and also in sorrow. Your faithfulness is my joy. In Your presence I find comfort and rest. You believe in me and encourage me to persevere. I know now that I am never alone in my battles. You give me a mighty armor for protection, and You lead me as I soldier on. I trust in You to deliver me out of my troubles and into a place of joyful singing. Oh Lord, build up my faith in You. Make it stronger! I want my trust in You to grow every day of my life. Amen.

Week 6
SHARING YOUR JOY

*These things have I spoken unto you,
that my joy might remain in you, and
that your joy might be full.*

JOHN 15:11

THE JOY OF SHARING

Dictionaries define *joy* as a state of perfect happiness. But Christians know that outside of Christ there is no such thing as perfect happiness. Joy is made perfect in Him. Jesus said, "If you keep my commands, you will remain in my love. . . . I have told you this so that my joy may be in you and that your joy may be complete" (John 15:10–11 NIV). This week's memory verse is similar. It reminds us to listen to and obey God's Word so our joy won't go dormant. Happiness is a fleeting emotion, but joy in the Lord is permanent. Jesus' joy grows and fills us. It is there through good times and bad.

Joy in the Lord is something we should share. Jesus told His disciples, "Go everywhere in the world, and tell the Good News to everyone" (Mark 16:15 NCV). The "Good News" is that true joy comes when we accept salvation through Christ. When we have that kind of joy, we want our friends and family to have it too. But spreading the Good News shouldn't stop there. As Christians, we are called to share our joy with everyone. We don't have to be missionaries or travel the world to be Christ's disciples. We can bring His joy into our homes, our workplaces, and our communities. We can teach Jesus' joy to little children through songs, stories, and play. We can bring joy to the elderly and sick through companionship and by reading scripture aloud to them and praying together. Volunteering to help anyone anywhere is another way to share our joy. So is being a reflection of Jesus' gentle and compassionate spirit in times of trouble and sadness.

In his sermon "Joy, a Duty," Charles Spurgeon wrote: "There is a marvelous medicinal power in joy. Most medicines are distasteful; but this, which is the best of all medicines, is sweet to the taste, and comforting to the heart. . .this blessed grace of joy is very contagious. . . . One dolorous spirit brings a kind of plague into the house; one person who is always wretched seems to stop all the birds singing wherever he goes; but, as the birds pipe to each other, and one morning songster quickens all the rest, and sets the groves ringing with harmony, so will it be with the happy cheerful spirit of a man who obeys the command of the text, 'Rejoice in the Lord always.' This grace of joy is contagious."

This week is about sharing your joy with others. As you give your joy away, the Lord will fill you up with even more. He makes this promise in Luke 6:38 (NKJV): "Give, and it will be given to you: good measure, pressed down, shaken together. . . . For with the same measure that you use, it will be measured back to you." Be generous with your joy. Give it to others wherever you go.

These things have I spoken unto you, that my joy might remain in you, and that your joy might be full.
JOHN 15:11

The Blank Page

You have spent the past five weeks reading and learning about joy. Along the way, you might have discovered that joy exists even in the most unlikely places. You have pondered joy and applied it to your daily life. Now spend time reflecting on what you have learned. Go back and look at each chapter heading. What have you learned about:

- God's pathway to joy?
- Finding joy in His creation?
- Striving for joy in your relationships?
- Experiencing joy when at work?
- God's deliverance through hard times?

Make notes about the ideas you have gleaned from each chapter. These will encourage and help you as you share your joy with others.

The Last Word

Have you memorized all six of the weekly memory verses? Here they are again.

Week One: "Thou wilt shew me the path of life: in thy presence is fulness of joy; at thy right hand there are pleasures for evermore" (Psalm 16:11).

Week Two: "This is the day which the LORD hath made; we will rejoice and be glad in it" (Psalm 118:24).

Week Three: "And be ye kind one to another, tenderhearted, forgiving one another, even as God for Christ's sake hath forgiven you" (Ephesians 4:32).

Week Four: "And whatsoever ye do, do it heartily, as to the Lord, and not unto men" (Colossians 3:23).

Week Five: "Thou art my hiding place; thou shalt preserve me from trouble; thou shalt compass me about with songs of deliverance" (Psalm 32:7).

This Week: "These things have I spoken unto you, that my joy might remain in you, and that your joy might be full" (John 15:11).

How does each verse speak to your heart? What have you done to incorporate these verses into your daily life? Think about ways you might share these scripture verses or their main ideas with others.

Week 6: DAY ONE

SHARE THE JOY OF NATURE

Job said, "Ask the animals, and they will teach you, or ask the birds of the air, and they will tell you. Speak to the earth, and it will teach you" (Job 12:7–8 NCV).

There are endless lessons found in nature. For example, someone discovered dogs could be trained to perform unique tasks. That person shared his discovery with the world, and today much joy comes from dogs trained to help police officers, aid and comfort the sick, elderly, or disabled, and even perform as entertainers.

Isaac Newton noticed an apple fall from a tree. It made him wonder why apples fall straight down and not sideways or otherwise. By questioning what he observed and after much thought and calculation, Newton discovered the law of gravity. Surely that brought him joy! He didn't keep his discovery to himself. He shared it with the world. Newton's discovery encouraged scientists who studied the earth and sky, which led to even more discoveries—and fun things like roller coasters.

Get in the habit of studying nature's lessons and connecting them with what you've learned from the Bible. You could compare today's stories of animals miraculously sensing danger and protecting their humans to God sending ravens to bring

Elijah food when Elijah ran and hid from King Ahab (see 1 Kings 17:4–6). God covers the sky with clouds, provides rain for the earth, and commands the wind (see Psalm 147:8). When you see these everyday weather occurrences you can connect them with God compassing the weather to fit His plan.

You can take what you learn from nature and give it to others along with a lesson from the Lord. Maybe you are a gardener and you've discovered your own secrets to growing amazing tomatoes. Share your discovery with friends at work. When they wonder how you grew such beautiful fruit, tell them you've learned to observe and question the little things God does, like how seeds grow and what makes plants strong. Or maybe you are a star-gazer and know all the constellations. The next time your child has a sleepover, take the children outside to look at the stars. Show them the constellations. Tell them God knows exactly how many stars there are, and He has a name for each one. Even little observations provide opportunities to share a Lord lesson with someone else: not one sparrow dies without God knowing (see Matthew 10:29). "The heavens declare the glory of God, and the skies announce what his hands have made" (Psalm 19:1 NCV).

Think of nature as God's classroom. As you learn from Him, share the joys of your discoveries with others. Use your discoveries to teach about God. Search the topic of "nature" in the Bible and apply what you read to your own observations. Everything in the natural world is His, and so much of it is filled with joyful discoveries worth sharing.

These things have I spoken unto you, that my joy
might remain in you, and that your joy might be full.
JOHN 15:11

The Blank Page

Make a plan to get your family interested in nature. Begin slowly by planning a visit to a nearby beach, a state park, or even the zoo. Plan ahead to make this a teachable event. Point out things you observe, and try to connect those things with something you've learned from the Bible.

As your family becomes more familiar with observing and interacting with nature, discuss ways you can share your love of nature with others. If animals are your passion, you could volunteer at a local animal shelter. If plants are your thing, plant a garden and share your harvest with a food bank. If you enjoy crafting with objects found in the great outdoors, share what you make with nursing home residents or, better yet, teach them to craft using leaves, pinecones, and other natural finds.

When your family shares the joy of nature with others, remind them to also share the idea of God as Creator. Every subtle mention of God and His creation, or connecting nature with a scripture verse or story from the Bible, could be a stepping-stone that leads someone to Christ.

The Last Word

Saint Francis of Assisi was a nature observer. This is obvious from the words he wrote for the familiar hymn "All Creatures of Our God and King."

"All creatures of our God and King, Lift up your voice and with us sing,
Alleluia! Alleluia!
Thou burning sun with golden beam, Thou silver moon with softer gleam!
O praise Him! O praise Him! Alleluia! Alleluia! Alleluia!
Thou rushing wind that art so strong, Ye clouds that sail in heav'n along,
O praise Him! Alleluia!
Thou rising moon, in praise rejoice, Ye lights of evening, find a voice!
Thou flowing water, pure and clear, Make music for thy Lord to hear,
O praise Him! Alleluia!"

Take a minute right now to praise God for His creations.

A JOYFUL, JESUS ATTITUDE

Every relationship you have in your lifetime is an opportunity to share joy. Think about that—every relationship. A relationship is simply the way in which two or more people connect. There are family relationships, friend relationships, relationships with classmates, coworkers, people at church, neighbors, strangers . . .the list goes on. With each connection, you make the choice to share joy, or not.

Sharing joy doesn't mean always wearing a smile and having a Pollyanna attitude. Joy is shared when you become a reflection of Christ. When you do your best to have a Jesus-like attitude, you can bring a little joy into almost any situation.

Maybe you know some negative people. Instead of preaching positivity to them, you could bring them joy and accentuate the positive by complimenting them on their good points and praising their accomplishments.

If someone is sad, instead of saying "Cheer up!" or giving advice, you could listen to that person's troubles and show compassion. The German pastor Dietrich Bonhoeffer said, "We must learn to regard people less in the light of what they do or omit to do, and more in the light of what they suffer." Compassion is like good medicine. It can bring joy to an aching heart.

When work becomes stressful and you and your coworkers fall off the happy cliff and into the valley of grumpiness, you need a pick-me-up. Bring in a special treat to share or load some funny videos on your laptop and offer to share them with coworkers during your breaks. Small acts of kindness and a brief respite of fun can help lift spirits, if only for a while.

At home when your family is in a slump, put on some happy music. Get into the habit of singing while you do housework. When you adjust your attitude to be a reflection of Christ, there is a better chance that your family members will adjust their attitudes as well.

You can hold a door open for a stranger, say a cheerful "hello," offer a sincere compliment, express thanks to a store employee . . .even the tiniest acts can bring someone joy.

Thomas à Kempis, a canon during the medieval period and author of a Christian devotional called "The Imitation of Christ," wrote: "The reflections on a day well spent furnish us with joys more pleasing than ten thousand triumphs." When you spend your day doing your best to share joy with others, God will fill your heart with His joy. The more of your joy you give, the more of His joy you get. You might never know how you brought joy into someone's day, but God knows. He saw every smile, heard each kind and uplifting word, and He was there when you showed compassion. Think about what you did today to share some Jesus joy. Then decide what you can do tomorrow to be an even better reflection of Him.

These things have I spoken unto you, that my joy might remain in you, and that your joy might be full.
JOHN 15:11

The Blank Page

Jesus said, "These things have I spoken unto you, that my joy might remain in you, and that your joy might be full" (John 15:11).

Today, ask yourself, *How well do I know the words of Jesus? What has He spoken to me through the Bible?*

All scripture, whether spoken by Jesus or not, is God-breathed—inspired by God (see 2 Timothy 3:16). When Jesus spoke, He spoke by the authority of His Father. When you read and meditate on the four Gospels (Matthew, Mark, Luke, and John), you not only learn what Jesus said, but you also see the way He lived and interacted with others. His life on earth provides a perfect example of how God wants you to be in all situations and in every relationship.

Don't just read about Jesus; study Him! Ponder His relationships with others. Then try to be more like Him. When you make Jesus the center of your life, when you allow Him to fill you with His wisdom, then your joy will be full, and others will begin to see Jesus through your actions and words.

The Last Word

When lottery winners are interviewed, they often say they want to use their prize money to help others. Many do just that. They help in big and small ways through charities, schools, community funds, grants. . . . That kind of sharing is wonderful, but so is sharing a joyful spirit.

A lottery winner in Wisconsin not only vowed to help others with his winnings; he went into the community and shared his joy with a stranger. The twenty-four-year-old winner went to a local department store, purchased a $200 gift card, and gave it randomly to a woman shopping there with her young children. The woman was skeptical. After all, who does that sort of thing! But finally, she trusted the young man's lottery story and his desire to share his joy. Instead of keeping the gift, the woman chose to pay it forward to a family she knew could benefit. "It would be a very cool blessing for their family," she said.

When you experience joy in your life, pay your joyful spirit forward. It doesn't have to be a gift of money. Just do something kind to share your joy! Then pray and ask God to continue to pay forward your gift of joy to bless someone else.

 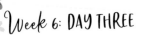

Jesus, His disciples, and a crowd of followers were leaving Jericho when they heard a blind beggar, Bartimaeus, shouting, "Jesus! Jesus! Have mercy on me!" Many of those following Jesus told Bartimaeus to be quiet. But Jesus said to His disciples, "Call him." When Bartimaeus heard, he ran to Jesus. "What do you want me to do for you?" Jesus asked. Bartimaeus said, "Rabbi, I want to see." Immediately, Bartimaeus received Jesus' gift of sight, and then he followed Jesus. (See Mark 10:46–52 NIV.) Reread that last sentence—when Bartimaeus received his sight, he followed Jesus.

Each day, God gifts us with miracles and mercies. We ask and beg Him for what we want, and He answers. What we do afterward is important. Like Bartimaeus, we should follow Jesus. He hears our calls, and now we need to listen for His. Jesus calls us to follow Him and do His work here on earth.

Volunteering is a great way to serve Jesus and also share with others the joy of knowing Him. Some volunteers travel to other countries to help the sick and poor. The Peace Corps, Habitat for Humanity, the Red Cross—these are just a few well-known organizations that recruit volunteers to serve others. But most volunteer opportunities happen at home through community service and the church.

There are many ways you can serve. Consider volunteering in a nursing facility. Bring joy to the residents there by reading aloud, leading sing-alongs, playing games. . . . Volunteer as a mentor for school-aged children. Provide rides for cancer patients to and from their treatments. Work in a food pantry. Visit sick or elderly shut-ins from your church. Teach Sunday school. Stuff envelopes. Work at special events. . . Be creative. Think of new ways to volunteer. Find a need and fill it. You can even start your own volunteer group.

Volunteering is sometimes hard work, and it can require hours of your time. But if your focus is on Jesus and sharing your joy of knowing Him, volunteer work will be one of the most rewarding activities you do. It can connect you with other Christians and provide opportunities for you to share Christ with those who don't know Him.

The refrain of an old hymn called "As a Volunteer" goes like this:

"A volunteer for Jesus,
A soldier true!
Others have enlisted,
Why not you?
Jesus is the Captain,
We will never fear;
Will you be enlisted
As a volunteer?"

If you call out to Jesus and ask Him to open your eyes to volunteer opportunities, He will lead you. All you have to do is answer His call and follow Him. Jesus is calling you to be a soldier in His army, to work as His disciple helping others and sharing the Good News. Will you answer His call? What can you do in your own community to share with others the joy of knowing Jesus?

These things have I spoken unto you, that my joy
might remain in you, and that your joy might be full.
JOHN 15:11

The Blank Page

Getting your children involved in serving others is a great way to ready them for a lifetime of caring, compassion, and the joy of working for Jesus. There are many ways your family can volunteer together. Here are ten ideas to get you started:

1. Help an elderly or sick person in your neighborhood. Volunteer to cut the grass, weed, rake leaves, or shovel snow. Keep your eyes open for other needs like painting or minor home repairs that you can do together.
2. Donate gently used clothing and toys to a local charity.
3. Once a month, shop together and fill a grocery bag to donate to a family in need.
4. Put together care packages to send to soldiers overseas. (Reach out to your local military and veterans' organizations to find out how you can help.)
5. Join charity walks that increase awareness and raise funds to fight specific illnesses.
6. Participate in community clean-up days.
7. Thank fire and rescue personnel by baking cookies and delivering them to the firehouse.
8. Make thank-you cards for police officers, crossing guards, and other community helpers.
9. If you have older children, work together setting up a fundraiser to provide clothing and other items for a local homeless shelter. Socks, underwear, and personal care items are always needed. Check with your local shelters for specific needs.
10. Organize a car wash, and donate the proceeds to a worthy cause.

The Last Word

You've used all six memory cards and applied the memory tips offered in this book to memorize six verses and apply them to your life. But your commitment to memorize scripture has just begun. Keep at it. Promise yourself and God that you will continue to memorize at least one verse each week.

The Bible speaks about God's words:

- "The word of the LORD is right" (Psalm 33:4).
- "Thy word is true from the beginning" (Psalm 119:160).
- "Every word of God is pure" (Proverbs 30:5).
- "For the word of God is quick, and powerful, and sharper than any twoedged sword" (Hebrews 4:12).
- "The entrance of thy words giveth light; it giveth understanding unto the simple" (Psalm 119:130).
- "Heaven and earth shall pass away, but my words shall not pass away" (Matthew 24:35).

There are many other scripture verses about the Word of God, but perhaps the most important is this: "Do not merely listen to the word, and so deceive yourselves. Do what it says" (James 1:22 NIV). You might also think of it this way: "Do not merely read the Bible. Memorize it!" Knowing what's in the Bible and using it every day is the key reason to memorize scripture. You can't apply what God tells you unless you remember His instructions.

Sometimes well-meaning friends cause more harm than good. They say too much, thinking their advice is helpful. Words carry heavy weight, and the wrong ones can make a bad situation even worse. Joy walks quietly, hand in hand with comfort when you think before you speak. Well-chosen words bring light into darkness. A hug and a few words are usually enough. "I'm here for you." "I'm sorry you have to go through this." "How can I help?" Listen without pushing your opinions. If responding to a death, it's okay to reminisce about the good things. Remembering them brings back feelings of joy.

Kind acts can also bring joy into a bad situation. Act on your words. Be there. Help with household chores, babysitting, making meals. Keep checking in. Do your best to be intuitive about what your friend needs.

People suffer differently. Some may want you to pray with them or hear comforting words from scripture. Others might not. If a person can't or won't pray, you can pray for them and rely on your own faith, asking God to intervene. Storm heaven with your prayers.

In times of sadness and trouble, joy is silent. It waits patiently and surfaces again when the time comes for healing. Recalling your acts of comfort and kindness might one day bring a smile to the receiver. The novelist Dinah Maria Mulock said, "Those whose own light is quenched are often the light-bringers." Who knows? The person you comforted might become a better comforter because of you.

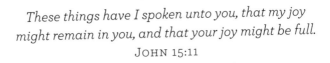

These things have I spoken unto you, that my joy
might remain in you, and that your joy might be full.
JOHN 15:11

The Blank Page

Providing hope is another way of bringing joy into a troubled situation. There is joy in knowing the Lord and trusting in Him as the source of deliverance. Following are scripture verses you can use when helping a friend through a difficult time. Add them to your memory list.

- "Blessed are they that mourn: for they shall be comforted" (Matthew 5:4).
- "In this world you will have trouble. But take heart! I have overcome the world" (John 16:33 NIV).
- "God is our refuge and strength, a very present help in trouble" (Psalm 46:1).
- "The lowly he sets on high, and those who mourn are lifted to safety" (Job 5:11 NIV).
- "But those who hope in the LORD will renew their strength. They will soar on wings like eagles; they will run and not grow weary, they will walk and not be faint" (Isaiah 40:31 NIV).
- "Cast thy burden upon the LORD, and he shall sustain thee: he shall never suffer the righteous to be moved" (Psalm 55:22).
- "But now, Lord, what do I look for? My hope is in you" (Psalm 39:7 NIV).
- "For whatever things were written before were written for our learning, that we through the patience and comfort of the Scriptures might have hope" (Romans 15:4 NKJV).

The Last Word

The French Impressionist painters Auguste Renoir and Henri Matisse were close friends. Renoir's health failed in the last years of his life, and he became almost paralyzed with arthritis. In spite of severe pain in his hands, Renoir continued to paint. Matisse visited Renoir daily. He watched his friend suffer and work. "Auguste," he said, "why do you continue to paint when you are in such agony?" Renoir kept painting. He answered, "The beauty remains. The pain passes."

This is also true of joy. Pain and suffering pass away, but joy in the Lord goes on. Do you remember this verse from Week 5? "When you pass through the waters, I will be with you; and through the rivers, they shall not overflow you. When you walk through the fire, you shall not be burned, nor shall the flame scorch you" (Isaiah 43:2 NKJV). Notice the words *pass through*. We *pass through* our troubles with God leading us. The pain passes. The beauty left behind remains in our memories and in other ways. The apostle Peter wrote that even though we go through trials in life, we can be truly glad because there is wonderful joy ahead (see 1 Peter 1:6–7). We might pass through a lifetime of trials, but there is joy in knowing the Lord, and the joy of heaven awaits those who believe.

SCRIPTURE, ANECDOTES, AND EXAMPLES

Maybe you wonder how to share the Bible with those who don't know the Lord. You worry about sounding too preachy or self-righteous. Don't worry! Jesus will guide you. When studying Him in the Gospels, you'll see that He sometimes quoted scripture, but He also used anecdotes and examples. You can do the same.

For example, you and a friend decide to train for a local 5K race. A few weeks into training, she becomes discouraged and thinks about quitting. You can encourage her and quote scripture by saying something like, "In the Bible, Paul says, 'Many runners enter a race, and only one of them wins the prize. So run to win!' Let's not give up. We can do this!" That brief sharing of scripture might open the door to a longer conversation about Paul, the Bible, or perseverance.

Maybe your spouse is tired of being the only one in your neighborhood who helps the elderly widow on your block. You might agree: "That's true. But don't forget what it says in Ecclesiastes 11:1." You've shown that you understand and also added a reminder of an encouraging verse from scripture.

Here is a humorous way to share scripture with a child who would rather sleep than get up. When you try to wake him or her, the conversation might go something like this:

You (with a gentle tap on the shoulder): "*Poof!* You are an ant!"

Child: "An aunt?!"

You: "You know. An ant, like a bug!"

Now you can share Proverbs 6:6–11. The book of Proverbs is filled with verses to memorize and interject into conversations.

You can begin with a teaser—telling just enough to catch a person's attention. Let's say one of your friends has just experienced a breakup, and she feels sad and alone. You could reassure her that you're there for her by saying, "You can count on me. I'll be your Ruth." That will surely lead to more conversation if your friend has never heard the story of Ruth and Naomi. If she's curious, you can tell her about Ruth and Naomi's friendship and also share with her the story's joyful ending.

Maybe rumors are flying at work about the possibility of layoffs. You could say, "I feel like King Nebuchadnezzar is about to throw us into the fire—but we know how that turned out." You've just used a writing technique—ending with a cliff-hanger! Your coworkers might be curious to know what on earth you are talking about. Who is this Nebuchadnezzar person? What about a fire? How *did* it turn out?

See? It's not so hard to share the Bible with others. You don't have to be preachy. But you do have to know the Bible well so you will be prepared with scripture verses, anecdotes, and examples to bring Jesus joy into the lives of your friends, family, and others.

These things have I spoken unto you, that my joy
might remain in you, and that your joy might be full.
JOHN 15:11

The Blank Page

Following are five situations you might encounter. Think about how you could incorporate a scripture verse, anecdote, or example from the Bible into a conversation.

- Your brother-in-law lost his job and has remained unemployed after six months of job searching.
- A friend's mother recently died after a long battle with cancer.
- Your coworkers feel discouraged because the boss favors one or two employees over the others.
- Your daughter is in the first year of high school and she has no idea what she wants to do with her life after she graduates.
- An elderly person you know complains to you about growing old.

The Last Word

There will be times when God leads you to share scripture straight from the Bible. He might also make you aware that someone you know is ready to receive Jesus Christ as their Lord and Savior. When you feel God nudging you in that direction, go there. Talk about Jesus joy—the joy found in accepting Him as Lord and Savior. Tell others about the Bible. Explain that it is the true and inspired Word of God. It holds God's answers to many of our questions.

Jesus gave His disciples the mission to evangelize, to bring the good news of salvation to the world. There are many ways to do it. The evangelist Theodore Epp said, "God has given believers the responsibility of spreading the Gospel to all the world, and we need to use all at our disposal to accomplish this task." Pray and ask God to lead you. Then in all situations keep your heart and mind open to hear His words. Trust Him to show you the best way to share your faith with others and lead them to finding joy in Jesus.

Week 6: DAY SEVEN
PUTTING IT ALL TOGETHER

You've come to the end of this six-week Bible memory devotional. Along with the verses on the scripture memory cards, you have also read and thought about many other verses you can add to your memory bank.

During the past six weeks, you discovered that joy can be found in all places. Finding it requires reading and memorizing God's Word, incorporating it into your daily life, and learning to perceive a glass as half-full instead of half-empty. You have learned to share with others Jesus' joy—the joy that comes from knowing Him. You found out that joy can be shared even in sadness and trouble. You've discovered ways to share the Bible with others without sounding preachy, and also that there are times to preach. You've come to understand that there are many ways to evangelize and lead others to the gift of salvation. Now you can use everything you've learned to share the inexpressible and glorious joy you've found knowing the Lord.

Gratefulness is one additional component to finding joy. In his letter to the Thessalonians, Paul wrote: "Rejoice always, pray continually, give thanks in all circumstances; for this is God's will for you in Christ Jesus" (1 Thessalonians 5:16–18 NIV). A scientific study of gratefulness published in the *Journal of Personality and*

COMFORT AND JOY

Job suffered. In a matter of hours his livestock, servants, and children died. In the midst of grieving Job became ill, his body covered with sores. "How I wish that God would answer my prayer and do away with me," he said. "Then I would be comforted, knowing that in all of my pain I have never disobeyed God" (Job 6:8–10 CEV). Job was not only a good man who suffered but a faithful one. Nothing would come between him and God, but still, like any human in his situation, Job sought relief.

"Why do you still trust God? Why don't you curse Him and die?" his wife told him. That certainly wasn't what Job needed. It didn't bring him relief.

Three of Job's friends came to comfort him, and like Job's wife they made things worse. Eliphaz reminded Job of times when Job had comforted others. Those words might have brought Job a morsel of joy—knowing he had been a source of comfort. But Eliphaz didn't stop there. He added that he doubted Job really understood the pain others suffered and suggested that Job must have committed an evil sin to make God angry. "That's why this happened to you, Job!" Job's other two friends, Bildad and Zophar, chimed in, agreeing. Zophar even hinted that whatever Job had done, he probably deserved to be punished even more. "Beg God for forgiveness, Job."

Social Psychology concluded that grateful people differ from those who don't practice gratefulness. "They are more empathic, forgiving, helpful, and supportive than are their less grateful counterparts. . . . People with stronger dispositions toward gratitude tend to be more spiritually and religiously minded. Grateful people are higher in positive emotions and life satisfaction and also lower in negative emotions such as depression, anxiety, and envy."[10] In other words, they are happier and more joyful.

This week's memory verse is Jesus speaking about the importance of paying close attention to His words. He says, "These things have I spoken unto you, that my joy might remain in you, and that your joy might be full" (John 15:11). Joy is knowing the Father, Son, and Holy Spirit. It grows through commitment, trust, faith, and gratefulness. Once you've found it, you have it! It will never run out.

There will be days when you don't feel joy, days when negativity creeps in. But on those days, you know that Satan is trying to steal your joy. You have the tools to stop him. Put them to good use. Keep this book close by, and revisit the devotionals whenever you feel joy slipping away. Reuse the scripture memory cards. Make some of your own. The joy you've found in Jesus is a precious and ongoing gift. Treat it well.

These things have I spoken unto you, that my joy might remain in you, and that your joy might be full.
JOHN 15:11

---

[10] Michael E. McCullough, Robert A. Emmons, and Jo-Ann Tsang, "The Grateful Disposition: A Conceptual and Empirical Topography," *Journal of Personality and Social Psychology* 82, no. 1 (2002): 124, https://greatergood.berkeley.edu/pdfs/GratitudePDFs/7McCullough-GratefulDisposition.pdf.

The Blank Page

Here are ten final questions to think about:

- What is joy?
- Where does joy come from?
- Where is the most unlikely place you have found joy?
- What can you do from today and onward to turn negative thinking positive?
- How can someone find joy in the midst of sadness or suffering?
- What does it mean to have Jesus joy?
- Why is scripture memorization important?
- What are three different ways to share scripture with others?
- How can joy improve your relationships?
- How can practicing joy improve you?

The Last Word

Dear God, thank You for being the source of my inexpressible and glorious joy. I praise You for the gift of life and the joy I find in living each day. I am grateful for the times You have opened my senses to the joys found in Your creation. Continue to show me, Lord. Make me aware of the fine details, the little joys all around me.

Father, I'm still learning to live a life filled with joy. Keep teaching me. Set Your words firmly in my heart so I can take them with me wherever I go. Remind me that joy exists in all circumstances. Cover me with Your armor of protection, and deliver me when Satan tries to steal my joy.

I want to be Your disciple, a missionary, Your ambassador to the world. Show me how. Guide me to share the joy of knowing You with everyone I meet, and help me to lead others to accept the joyful gift of salvation through Christ. In the name of Your Son, Jesus, I pray, amen.

THOU WILT SHEW ME THE PATH OF LIFE: IN THY PRESENCE IS FULNESS OF JOY; AT THY RIGHT HAND THERE ARE PLEASURES FOR EVERMORE.

PSALM 16:11

This is the day which
the Lord hath made; we will
rejoice and be glad in it.

PSALM 118:24

AND BE YE KIND ONE TO ANOTHER,
TENDERHEARTED, FORGIVING ONE
ANOTHER, EVEN AS GOD FOR CHRIST'S
SAKE HATH FORGIVEN YOU.

EPHESIANS 4:32

And whatsoever ye do,
do it heartily, as to the
Lord, and not unto men.

COLOSSIANS 3:23